THE
FRENCH
WAY

LA FRANCE

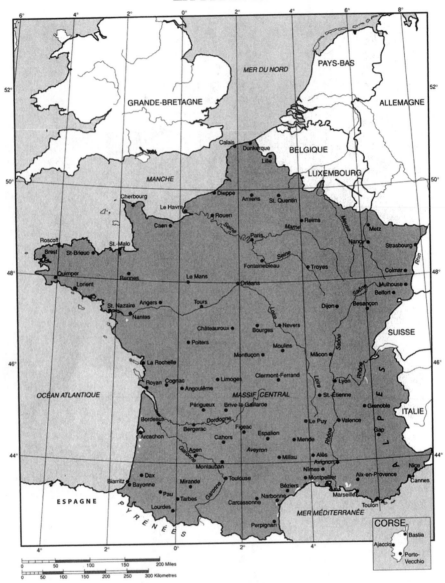

PAYS-BAS

MER DU NORD

GRANDE-BRETAGNE

ALLEMAGNE

Calais
Dunkerque
Lille
BELGIQUE
LUXEMBOURG

MANCHE

Cherbourg
Dieppe
Amiens St. Quentin
Le Havre
Rouen
Reims
Metz
Caen
Paris
Marne
Nancy
Strasbourg
Roscoff
St.-Malo
Brest St-Brieuc
Seine
Colmar
Quimper
Fontainebleau
Troyes
Mulhouse
Rennes
Le Mans
Belfort
Lorient
Orléans
Besançon
St. Nazaire Angers
Tours
Dijon
Nantes
Loire
Châteauroux
Bourges
Nevers
SUISSE
Poitiers
Moulins
La Rochelle
Montluçon
Mâcon
Royan Cognac
Limoges
Clermont-Ferrand
Lyon
OCÉAN ATLANTIQUE
Angoulême
MASSIF CENTRAL
St.-Étienne
Périgueux
Brive-la-Gaillarde
Grenoble
ITALIE
Bordeaux
Dordogne
Le Puy Valence
Gap
Bergerac
Figeac
Espalion
Arcachon
Cahors
Mende
Agen
Aveyron
Millau
Alès
Nice
Montauban
Avignon
Dax
Mirande
Toulouse
Nîmes
Aix-en-Provence
Cannes
Biarritz
Bayonne
Montpellier
Pau
Tarbes
Béziers
Marseille
Lourdes
Narbonne
Toulon
Carcassonne
ESPAGNE
PYRÉNÉES
MER MÉDITERRANÉE
Perpignan

SUISSE
ITALIE
ALPES
Rhône
Saône
Doubs
Rhin
Meuse
Garonne
Isère

CORSE
Bastia
Ajaccio
Porto-Vecchio

OCÉAN ATLANTIQUE
ESPAGNE

0   50   100   150   200 Miles
0   50   100 150 200 250 300 Kilometres

The Keys to the Behavior, Attitudes,
and Customs of the French

THE

FRENCH
WAY

Second Edition

ROSS STEELE

Recipient of France's highest award, The *Légion d'Honneur*

McGraw·Hill

New York   Chicago   San Francisco   Lisbon   London   Madrid   Mexico City
Milan   New Delhi   San Juan   Seoul   Singapore   Sydney   Toronto

The **McGraw·Hill** Companies

Library of Congress Cataloging-in-Publication Data

Steele, Ross.
    The French way : the keys to the behavior, attitudes, and customs of the
French / Ross Steele.
        p.   cm.
    Includes bibliographical references and index.
    ISBN 0-07-142807-0
        1. France—Social life and customs.   2. National characteristics, French.
    I. Title.

    DC34.S74   2006
    305.8009444—dc22   2005056287

1 2 3 4 5 6 7 8 9 0   FGR/FGR   0 9 8 7 6

ISBN 0-07-142807-0

Artwork on page 61 by Fred Dolven; page 92 by Mapping Specialists

McGraw-Hill books are available at special quantity discounts to use as premiums and sales
promotions, or for use in corporate training programs. For more information, please write to
the Director of Special Sales, Professional Publishing, McGraw-Hill, Two Penn Plaza, New York,
NY 10121-2298. Or contact your local bookstore.

Also in this series:

Flippo: *The German Way*

Noble and Lacasa: *The Hispanic Way*

Contantino and Gambella: *The Italian Way*

Tadaka and Lampkin: *The Japanese Way*

Dabars: *The Russian Way,* Second Edition

By the same author:

When in France, Do as the French Do

This book is printed on acid-free paper.

CONTENTS

CONTENTS

PREFACE TO THE SECOND EDITION

This is a completely revised edition of *The French Way,* covering events including the May 2005 referendum in which the French rejected the proposed constitution for the European Union and the rioting that lasted three weeks in the suburbs of Paris and other major French cities in October and November 2005.

The number of articles has increased from eighty-five to ninety. All of the original articles have been revised and updated to include, among other recent events, the opening of the magnificent **Viaduc de Millau;** the launch of the world's largest passenger plane, the 555-seat, double-deck **Airbus 380**; and the beginning of the free digital television network **TNT**. Among the new articles are ***Vive la différence!*** and Population, which gives a detailed overview of French society based on the 2004 census.

INTRODUCTION

In Thomas Jefferson's opinion, "Every man has two countries: his own and France." France's cities, villages, and picturesque countryside, her medieval cathedrals, castles, and art museums, her restaurants, high-fashion and luxury goods are admired throughout the world. But who are the French? Foreigners have many different views of them, both positive and negative.

This book takes a new look at today's French society through some characteristic French behaviors, attitudes, and customs. During recent times, many traditional French values have been buffeted by the winds of change, which have produced deep tensions within the social groups caught up in the process of modernization, the greater influence of the European Union on daily life, and the globalization of economic forces. The tension between nationalism and internationalism, for example, has erupted onto the world stage as France has adopted an independent position in political and economic debates in international forums. This has led to criticisms of French arrogance. On the other hand, France has consistently pursued a policy of promoting world peace, humanitarian aid through the NGO **Médecins Sans Frontières** (Doctors Without Borders), and economic aid programs by wealthy nations in developing countries.

Foreigners looking at France from the viewpoint of their own cultural values often misunderstand French reactions and perceive contradictions in the collective behavior of the French. This book helps to clear up such misunderstandings by placing French behavior and attitudes in their own context and explaining why long-standing traditions within France give coherence to French reactions when seen from within their society. Readers will acquire greater awareness of similarities and differences between their cultural traditions and those of the French. This knowledge will increase their capacity to communicate appropriately with the French and enjoy their company. On a personal level, the French can be the most charming of acquaintances and the most loyal of friends. Above all, they are individuals in a country where individualism is a national characteristic.

Alexis de Tocqueville wrote in 1865 that "The French are both the most brilliant and most dangerous of all European nations, and the best qualified to become, in the eyes of other peoples, an object of admiration, hatred, compassion, or alarm—never of indifference." Many foreigners today still share this opinion. The French continue to surprise, frustrate, amuse, and stimulate the world.

1. ABBREVIATIONS AND ACRONYMS

Abbreviations have entered the daily vocabulary of the French. Tourists will need to recognize these:

Transportation

RATP	**Régie autonome des transports parisiens**
	Autonomous administration of Parisian transportation; the Paris metro, RER, and bus system
RER	**Réseau Express Régional**
	Paris and suburban-to-suburban rapid rail transport system
RN	**Route nationale**
	National road
SNCF	**Société Nationale des Chemins de Fer Français**
	National syndicate of railroads; the national rail system
TEE	**Trans-Europ-Express**
	Trans-Europe express train
TGV	**Train à grande vitesse**
	High-speed train
VAL	**Véhicule automatique léger**
	Light automatic vehicle; driverless metro train
VTT	**Vélo tout-terrain**
	Mountain bike

European and International Institutions

ALENA	**Accord de libre-échange nord américain**	
	North American Free Trade Agreement (NAFTA)	
EURO (€)	**Unité monétaire européenne**	
	European currency	
GATT	**Accord général sur les tarifs douaniers et le commerce**	
	General Agreement on Tariffs and Trade	
ONU	**Organisation des Nations Unies**	
	United Nations (UN)	
OTAN	**Organisation du Traité de l'Atlantique du Nord**	
	North Atlantic Treaty Organization (NATO)	
PAC	**Politique agricole commune**	
	Common agricultural policy	
UE	**Union européenne**	
	European Union	

French Institutions

ANPE	**Agence nationale pour l'emploi**	
	National unemployment agency	
BNP Paribas	**Banque nationale de Paris Paribas**	
	A major national bank	
CFDT	**Confédération française démocratique du travail**	
	A center-left trade union	
CGT	**Confédération générale du travail**	
	A previously Communist trade union	
DOM-TOM	**Départements et territoires d'outre-mer**	
	Overseas administrative districts and territories	
EDF	**Electricité de France**	
	The partly state-owned electricity company	
ENA	**École nationale d'administration**	
	National higher education school for public servants	
GDF	**Gaz de France**	
	The partly state-owned natural gas company	
MEDEF	**Mouvement des entreprises de France**	
	Agency representing CEOs of large companies	

P et T	**Postes et télécommunications**
	The French post office
RF	**République française**
	French Republic
SG	**Société générale**
	A major national bank

Daily Life

BA	**Bonne action**
	Good deed
BCBG	**Bon chic, bon genre**
	Typical elegant bourgeois look
BD	**Bande dessinée**
	A cartoon or comic book; literally, "drawn strip"
BP	**Boîte postale**
	Mailbox
CRS	**Compagnies Républicaines de Sécurité**
	Republican Companies of Safety; the riot police
FNAC	**Fédération Nationale d'Achat des Cadres**
	Discount chain of book, music, and computer stores
HT	**Hors taxes**
	Tax free
HLM	**Habitation à loyer modéré**
	Low-rent dwelling, cheap high-rise apartment building
JO	**Jeux olympiques**
	Olympic Games
JT	**Journal télévisé**
	Television news broadcast
OGM	**Organismes (végétaux) génétiquement modifiés**
	Genetically modified (GM) foods
PACS	**Pacte civil de solidarité**
	Civil union
PDG	**Président-directeur général**
	Chief executive officer (CEO) of a firm
PMU	**Pari mutuel urbain**
	The state horse-race betting agency

PV	**Procès-verbal (Contravention)**	
	Parking ticket	
RTT	**Réduction du temps de travail**	
	Leave days associated with the thirty-five-hour workweek	
RMI-RMA	**Revenu minimum d'insertion–Revenu minimum d'activité**	
	Financial allowance paid by the state to the unemployed looking for work	
SAMU	**Service d'aide médicale d'urgence**	
	Twenty-four-hour urgent ambulance service	
SMIC	**Salaire minimum interprofessionnel de croissance**	
	Minimum wage	
SVP	**S'il vous plaît**	
	Please	
TTC	**Toutes taxes comprises**	
	All taxes included	
TNT	**Télévision numérique terrestre**	
	Digital television	
TVA	**Taxe à la valeur ajoutée**	
	Value-added tax	
VF	**Version française (d'un film)**	
	A movie with a dubbed French soundtrack	
VO	**Version originale (d'un film)**	
	A movie with the original language soundtrack	
VPC	**Vente par correspondance**	
	Mail order	

2. ACCENTS AND LANGUAGE

French is spoken with a different accent in different parts of France. The rapid, taut Parisian accent is very different from the twangy, nasal accent in the **Midi** (the south of France), which—if we are to believe the southerners—reflects their jovial personality and their sunny climate.

As with all languages, the spoken language evolves more rapidly than the written language. Cardinal Richelieu (1585–1642) established the **Académie française** in 1635 to stabilize and perfect the French language. Today, you will hear many colloquial and slang expressions that the forty elected-for-life members of the **Académie française** refuse to include in their dictionary, which rules over the correctness of the French language. Many words in French have a Greek or Latin origin. Greek or Latin roots are frequently combined with Greek or Latin prefixes and suffixes to coin new French words, such as **autoroute** or **télévision**.

Generally, the French have a conservative attitude toward the written language and take pride in their knowledge of its complexities. A majority of French people have opposed recent official attempts to modernize spelling. A hugely popular annual competition called **Les Dicos d'Or** (The Golden Dictionaries), conducted by Bernard Pivot, a former host of France's top literary television show, selects the best national spellers in a dictation test. French spelling is made even more difficult by gender and grammatical agreements.

The language spoken in the suburbs around major cities by the young generation of **beurs** (French-born children of immigrants from the North African countries of Algeria, Morocco, and Tunisia) is having a strong influence on nonstandard spoken French. **Verlan** is another form of spoken French popular among young people. They invert the syllables in a word so that **Arabe** becomes **beur**, **femme** (woman) becomes **meuf**, and **laisse tomber** (forget it) becomes **laisse béton**.

In addition to speaking French, people in some regions of France also speak a language that has for centuries expressed the region's cultural identity. The most spoken regional languages are **Breton** (in Brittany), **Occitan** (in southwestern France), and **Corsican** (in Corsica).

The first English word to enter the French language was "acre" in 1125. Since then, the French have borrowed many English words, but their pronunciation and often their meaning have changed—English speakers don't always recognize them in French conversation. The number of borrowed English words has increased greatly in recent decades as a result of the rapid growth of American pop culture, technology, computerization, and business management practices. New examples are **le show business, les people** (celebrities), **le management, le debriefing, la stock-option,** and **l'email** (instead of **le courriel**).

The language of France has always been **une affaire d'État** (a state affair). Alarmed by the lack of precision in usage and the loss of the "purity" of the French language that resulted from borrowed Anglo-American words and syntax, the government in 1966 established the **Haut Comité de la Langue Française**, a commission under the prime minister's control. Its mission was to defend French against the linguistic invasion of English by creating French words to replace English ones and to discourage the use of **franglais** (a mixture of French and English). Legislation passed in 1975 makes it obligatory to give a translation of foreign words or phrases used in advertisements. In 1994, the French parliament passed the Toubon law to expand on the 1975 law, making it mandatory to use the French language in official circulars, all public notices, and advertisements in France. Nonetheless, some major French international companies like Renault, Airbus, and BNP Paribas conduct management meetings in English.

Since 2005, English has been taught in French primary schools. English is the language used on 52 percent of all websites; 4.6 percent are in French. To increase the use of French on websites, the **Bibliothèque Nationale de France** or **BNF** (French National Library) did not accept the search engine Google's cost-free offer in 2005 to digitize the collections of the major world libraries. Instead, the French government assumed the huge cost of financing a "French Google" (**Google à la française**) to digitize the collections in the **BNF**.

3. AMERICANIZATION

For a long time, the French have been fascinated by the skyscrapers of New York, Hollywood Westerns, and American business schools whose methods were seen as the key to new economic prosperity. The older generation also remembers with gratitude the bravery of the G.I.s who helped liberate France at the end of World War II. The G.I.s brought with them jazz music and American customs, like chewing gum. (Incidentally, the French are now the largest per capita consumers of chewing gum in the world.)

France has had historical links with America since the French explorer Samuel de Champlain founded the city of Québec in 1608 and the colony **Nouvelle France** (New France) was established. When the British army defeated the French near Québec in 1759, many French settlers migrated south to "Acadia" (New Brunswick and parts of the other maritime provinces) and along the Mississippi to Louisiana, which had been named in honor of King Louis XIV. In 2003, Louisiana, where part of the population still speaks French and Cajun, commemorated the bicentenary of the purchase of Louisiana by the United States from France.

The increasing domination of popular culture by American pop and rock music, television programs, and movies has provoked a hostile reaction from more traditional French people in the name of respect for national cultures and identities. The opening of the Euro Disney theme park in 1992 at Marne-la-Vallée, 32 kilometers east of Paris, focused the debate on the survival of French cultural traditions. The Disney theme park corporate values were criticized as an example of the homogenization of culture. Initially, this attack kept the number of French visitors below budgeted expectations. To attract more visitors, Disney broke with its corporate code of not serving alcoholic drinks and allowed wine to be served with meals, which is a French tradition. A name change to Disneyland Paris and the opening of the Walt Disney Studios Park in addition to the Disneyland Park have made this the most popular theme park in Europe today, but only 40 percent of the visitors are French.

The proliferation of fast-food outlets, such as McDonald's (**McDo** in colloquial French), has been perceived as a takeover of French life by American values. Despite this, the McDonald's chain now has over a thousand restaurants in France. They are popular with young people as well as white-collar workers, who make up 43 percent of their customers. They have also adapted to French customs by serving, in addition to hamburgers, a **McDo** version of the **croque-monsieur** (ham and cheese grilled on toast), Dannon yogurts for dessert, and, in addition to Coca-

Cola, Orangina and Kronenbourg beer. Nonetheless, McDonald's is seen by radical French farmers as a symbol of undesirable American world domination. For José Bové, the high-profile antiglobalization leader of Farmers' Union, McDonald's symbolizes **la malbouffe** (bad eating). In 2002, he and a group of farmers destroyed a McDonald's restaurant in the French town of Millau as part of a campaign against American support for genetically modified food, which the farmers wanted banned in France.

The January 2004 opening of the first Starbucks in France (on the Avenue de l'Opéra in the heart of Paris) sparked another heated controversy about the clash of American and French cultures. Starbucks was accused of being a sterile, nonsmoking, no alcohol environment serving poor quality coffee in Styrofoam cups. In contrast, the traditional French **café** has been a friendly place for people to meet, talk, and smoke if they wish, serving strong espresso in cups and saucers, light meals, and a full range of alcoholic drinks. Ten Starbucks had opened in Paris by the end of 2004.

When the twin towers of the World Trade Center in New York were destroyed by a terrorist attack on 11 September 2001, Jean-Marie Colombani, director of the influential **Le Monde** newspaper, wrote "We are all Americans now," and a large majority of French people agreed. However, anti-Americanism became strident again in 2003. When French president Jacques Chirac and German chancellor Gerhard Schroeder opposed the American-led war to liberate Iraq from the dictator Saddam Hussein, they became populist heroes in their countries. Defense Secretary Donald Rumsfeld's description of European countries that opposed the Iraq war as "old Europe" fueled the anti-American feelings of European protesters. The reaction in the United States was a massive boycott of French products.

The French are not fundamentally anti-American. While continuing to criticize American cultural imperialism, American unilateralism, and American-driven globalization, they flock to American movies (more than half the movie tickets sold in 2003 were to American movies) and to McDonald's. The United States is a popular French tourist destination and, in 2003, two hundred and sixty thousand French nationals became residents there.

4. ANGLO-SAXON

The French often use the term **Anglo-Saxon** pejoratively as a collective description of all English speakers from countries historically influenced by British culture. The centuries of rivalry between France and Great Britain that began with the Hundred Years' War (1337–1453) explain negative attitudes toward the British, as in the expressions **filer à l'anglaise** (literally, to take British leave, but expressed in English as "to take French leave") and **la perfide Albion** (treacherous Britain), apparently originally used by French sailors who were disoriented by the similarity between the English cliffs of Dover and the French cliffs of Calais on the English Channel (**la Manche**). The English say "Pardon my French" when they use crude language and call the French "Froggies" because they eat frogs. The French retaliate by calling the English **les Rosbeefs** because they like eating roast beef.

Anglo-Saxons in general and the English in particular are seen by the French as cold and aloof, whereas their own Latin temperament is considered far superior. Americans are distinguished as a separate group among Anglo-Saxons, but both Americans and the English are often seen in a popular stereotype as plotting together against French influence in world affairs.

5. ANIMALS

The French are a nation of animal lovers. With sixty-eight million pets for a population of sixty-two million, France has the highest percentage of pets in Europe. In 53 percent of French homes, you will find at least one pet. The high proportion of pet-owning homes seems especially surprising given the large number of French families who live in apartments, but then French city dwellers have strong links with rural France, where pets are traditional.

There are 36.7 million pet fish (**poissons**), 9.7 million cats (**chats**), and 8.6 million dogs (**chiens**). In Paris, there are more dogs than children, and tourists complain about dog poop in the streets. The affectionate words for "a cat" and "a dog" are **un minet** and **un toutou**. The poodle is the most popular breed of dog, followed by the labrador and the German shepherd. The favorite names for purebred dogs are Robert and Marcel. The French are allowed to take their pet dogs with them into **cafés** and restaurants. There are 8 million pet birds (**oiseaux**). Asnières, a suburb of Paris, has a famous pet cemetery.

The Society for the Protection of Animals (**SPA**) takes care of abandoned pets. The actor Brigitte Bardot (1934–) has campaigned for the need to protect animals (especially seals) from human cruelty and has established a foundation for this purpose.

6. *BLEU-BLANC-ROUGE*

Blue, white, and red are the colors of the French flag, which is also called **le Tricolore** (three colors). The flag dates from the French Revolution and replaced the flag of the monarchy, which was adorned with the **fleur de lys** (lily). The lily's color, white, was the royal color and blue and red were the colors of Paris, which the Marquis de La Fayette proposed combining in the Revolutionaries' tricolor cockade to symbolize the union of the monarchy and the people. Perhaps coincidentally, the same colors were those of a sister revolutionary nation for whose establishment de La Fayette had fought a few years earlier—the United States of America.

The **fleur de lys** is today the symbol of Québec and can be seen on the Québec flag and on car registration plates with the inscription **Je me souviens** (I remember [my French origins]).

French national sports teams wear blue when they compete internationally and are called **les Bleus** (the Blues) or **les Tricolores.**

7. BOURGEOISIE

The bourgeoisie, the urban middle class, grew in power and importance during the nineteenth century as a result of the 1789 Revolution, which put an end to the privileges of the nobility who had dominated French society until that time. Because membership in the true nobility depended solely on being born in that social class and not on personal merit or achievements, the Revolutionaries considered the nobility's privileges unjust.

The power of the nobility was shattered by the Revolution. The new wealthy class was the bourgeoisie, which provided the bankers, traders, and shopkeepers for the economic growth of post–Revolutionary France. They increased the political power they had won in the 1789 Revolution by supplying the educated workforce needed for the expanding administrative bureaucracy. In addition to their wealth, the bourgeoisie achieved social prestige by marrying members of the impoverished nobility. The Industrial Revolution further increased their wealth and influence.

The vast French middle class has continued to impose its values and tastes on society despite opposition from two groups: the working class, which became more politically organized through trade unions and the Communist and Socialist parties, and the intellectual class, which expressed contempt for the bourgeois obsession with money and materialistic goals. The growth of the liberal professions (doctors, lawyers, etc.) and of senior management in industry and commerce expanded the top echelons of the bourgeoisie during **les trente glorieuses**, the thirty years of rapid economic growth in France after World War II. During this period, the traditional bourgeois attitude of spending little and saving as much money as possible changed under pressure from the consumer society. A generation of affluent, professionally successful men and women emerged, the "new bourgeoisie" (**la nouvelle bourgeoisie**). Unlike preceding generations, they were not afraid to use credit to purchase consumer and luxury goods that were not essential but enhanced their lifestyle. The glossy magazine sold with *Le Figaro* (newspaper) on Saturdays reflects the tastes and aspirations of affluent professionals. The expression **BCBG** (**Bon chic, bon genre**), describes the conservative, elegantly dressed look of the well-off bourgeoisie and their air of respectability.

In the 1990s, a new group emerged within this class called **les bobos**, the colloquial expression for **les bourgeois bohèmes** (trendy bourgeois). They are bourgeois in the social and financial sense but unhappy with the traditional attitudes of their class. They prefer to buy and renovate apartments in the nonbourgeois areas of Paris and vote for the Socialists and Greens instead of for the conservative parties.

It has been said that in today's France, the old aristocracy has given way to a new one that controls the political, economic, intellectual, and social power of the nation. This elite bourgeoisie is made up of the leaders in politics, industry, management, public administration, and the liberal professions. Their power is based on family connections, success, and wealth. Their values are predominantly conservative and nationalistic. They are **les gens bien** (the admirable people), whose attitudes, fashions, and lifestyles are copied by the lower social classes. Two centuries after the Revolution, a strong social hierarchy remains with the upper levels of the bourgeoisie having replaced the nobility at the top of the hierarchy.

8. *BRANCHÉ*

Branché is a popular adjective used to describe a person whose behavior or attitudes are in keeping with or ahead of the latest trends—for example, **il est très branché** or **elle est très branchée**. **Branché** can also describe a trendy, fashionable place or product—for example, **un restaurant branché** or **un film branché**. Expressions with an equivalent meaning are **à la mode**, **dans le vent**, and the colloquial **cool**.

9. BREAD AND PASTRIES

Although bread is now sold in supermarkets, the French **boulangerie** (bakery) remains indispensable to the French way of life. Local bakers owe their comfortable survival to two facts, one historical and the other culinary/cultural. The historical fact is associated with Queen Marie-Antoinette; the culinary/cultural fact is the taste and aroma of the bread itself. The **baguette** is one of France's most cherished national symbols.

Bread retains enormous political significance since Queen Marie-Antoinette (1755–93), on being told that the people had no bread during the French Revolution, allegedly replied, "Well, then, let them eat cake!" From 1789 to the present day, no French government would dare allow the price of bread to climb out of reach of the poorest French family, although the price varies depending on the quality.

French bread in the local **boulangerie** is baked fresh several times a day and stales perceptibly by the following day. No French meal is complete without bread, not even breakfast, which commonly consists of nothing more than the leftover bread from the night before and a bowl of coffee or hot chocolate. Jam and butter usually accompany the bread at breakfast. On special occasions, croissants are bought.

The name of the long crusty French breadstick indicates its thickness and weight: **la ficelle** is the thinnest; then come **la baguette** (the most common), **la flûte**, and **le pain**. At meals, the breadstick is broken into pieces by hand and eaten without butter. For lunch in a **café**, a **baguette** can be cut in half and sliced lengthwise to make **un sandwich** filled with **pâté**, cheese, or ham.

Over the past decade, specialist **boulangeries** selling a wide range of types and country-style shapes of bread have become popular. The master breadmaker Lionel Poilâne, for whom bread was "the soul of civilization," acquired international fame with his **pain Poilâne**, a large, thick-crusted, circular sourdough loaf.

Local **boulangeries** sell croissants and simple pastries like **un chausson aux pommes** (apple-filled pastry). French pastry shops (**pâtisseries**) may sell bread in addition to their mouth-watering range of cakes, tarts, and elaborate pastries. Many pastries have religious or historical connotations—such as **une religieuse**, a chocolate éclair shaped to resemble a nun; **une madeleine**, a cake named after a nineteenth-century pastry cook and made famous by the novelist Marcel Proust (1871–1922), who discovered that it recalled his childhood memories; or **la tarte Tatin**, a caramelized apple tart named after restaurant owner Madame Tatin. A French schoolchild with a few euros to spend might stop at **la pâtisserie** on the way home from school to buy **un petit pain au chocolat**, a bun of flaky pastry with a slice of chocolate baked in the middle.

On Sunday mornings, **les pâtisseries** do a brisk trade in cakes (**gâteaux**) and fruit tarts (**tartes aux fruits**), which are bought as dessert for the family Sunday lunch. For weddings and christenings, **une pièce montée**, a tall cone-shaped arrangement of caramelized **profiteroles**, is the traditional pastry cake served to guests.

10. BRIDGES AND TUNNELS

The ancient stone bridges across the Seine in Paris (the oldest is, ironically, the **Pont Neuf** (New Bridge), built between 1578 and 1604), together with the banks of the Seine, have been part of the romantic image of Paris since Maurice Chevalier's (1888–1972) famous song **"Sous les ponts de Paris"** ("Under the Bridges of Paris"). The thirty-seventh Paris bridge across the Seine, a footbridge linking the Parc de Bercy to the Bibliothèque Nationale François Mitterrand, is planned for 2006 with the name Simone de Beauvoir. Another historic bridge, built between 1177 and 1185 by Saint Bénézet and his disciples across the river Rhône at Avignon, has been made famous by a traditional children's song **"Sur le Pont d'Avignon"** ("On the Bridge of Avignon"). The most ancient bridge in France is the tiered **Pont du Gard**, built to the height of 49 meters above the river Gard by the Romans as an aqueduct to bring water to the town of Nîmes in the south of France.

Contemporary French bridges and tunnels have been used as symbols of French engineering prowess, projecting an international image of modern industrial France whose achievements are not limited to arts and culture. Examples are the **Pont de Tancarville** (1959), suspended 47 meters above the Seine in Normandy; the **Pont de Normandie** (1995), at the mouth of the Seine between Le Havre and Honfleur, which is as long as the Champs-Élysées in Paris and is one of the largest cable bridges in the world; the highest bridge in the world, rising 343 meters above the river Tarn in southwestern France, the **Viaduc de Millau** (2004), designed by the English architect Sir Norman Foster and creating a direct route between Paris and the Mediterranean coast; the tunnel under Mont Blanc in the Alps (1965), linking France and Italy; and the Euro Tunnel under the English Channel (1994) between Calais and Folkestone, which allows the superfast Eurostar train to make the journey from Paris to London in three hours.

11. BUSINESS

Every country has a distinctive business culture. When you arrive in an American office for a business appointment, you are offered coffee. In France, you are not offered anything to drink. The American business office has a comfortable atmosphere, with paintings or prints on the wall, plants, reference books, a family photograph, and a discrete nameplate on the desk facing the visitor. It is an extension of home. In France, offices are often cramped and don't have these friendly features. American male executives wear suits but will receive visitors with their jackets off. The French are more formal. They don't take their jackets off, although middle managers often wear sports coats. Americans hand over their business cards immediately. The French prefer to give out business cards at the end of a meeting.

The French begin a business negotiation with a series of general considerations and statements before getting down to details. For example, they want to discuss the general business climate, economic trends, market conditions, and competing companies and their turnovers before discussing the financial details of the sale or profits to be made from the proposal. Americans tend to concentrate much earlier in a conversation on the "bottom line" details of how to reduce costs and increase profits from the deal under negotiation. Americans who are used to adopting a more pragmatic approach can find the intellectual approach of the French unsettling.

Americans also tend to proceed more rapidly to wrap up a deal and give more importance to the details of the final written agreement, setting out strict conditions if things go wrong. The French place more value on the unwritten agreement and on the goodwill of both parties. In addition to the financial details, they need to have a good feeling about the people and company they are negotiating with and are prepared to take more on trust. They tend not to follow such strict procedures in reviewing a proposal and thus may appear disorganized to Americans focused on rapid outcomes. It would be a mistake to imagine that the French behavior arises from any lack of thoroughness in checking details before reaching a decision. They simply follow different paths, which take longer and can frustrate time-conscious Americans.

French people sometimes interpret American directness as brusqueness. The French are more diplomatic. They don't like confrontation and don't like to lose face. Instead of giving a direct "no," they will, for example, suggest a need for more information. Foreigners need to understand French body language to be able to interpret what is not said. For the French, it's important for things to look good up front.

France has many **Écoles de commerce** (business schools), often associated with a local chamber of commerce. The top business school is the

École des Hautes Études Commerciales (HEC), which is one of the leading Grandes Écoles (see Education). Many senior executives in French industry and nationalized companies, however, have not attended a business school but have instead a math and science background from a famous Grande École, the École Polytechnique (X) or have graduated from the other famous Grande École, which is for civil servants, the École Nationale d'Administration (ENA). Intercompany dealings often take their cue, in fact, from the hierarchy of the school system, and a proposal may succeed largely because the negotiators attended the same Grande École. When the growth of consumerism and international trade in the 1960s and 1970s caused France to modernize its business culture, French students began going to the United States to add a business diploma to their training. Some Americans go to study in Europe, which shares with the United States a basically similar model of capitalism and where most American multinational corporations have offices or plants. The French economy is the world's sixth largest, coming after the United States, Japan, Germany, which has the biggest economy in the European Union, China, and Great Britain. A few major French corporations are still state controlled.

Golf and parties are less frequent forms of corporate entertainment in France than in the United States. The French use lunches and dinners to get to know their clients and to formalize the conclusion of an agreement. While an American businessperson might invite a client to his or her home for an informal family meal, in France, business meals take place in restaurants and conversation about family topics is infrequent. In this, there is, however, a difference between Paris and the provinces, where a warmer personal relationship is established and the client may be invited to meet the executive's family.

Business activity slows down considerably during the month of August, which is—along with July—the traditional time for vacation. Some industrial plants shut down, many companies maintain only skeletal staffing, and small shopkeepers in the cities hang a sign on their doors that reads Fermé pour vacances annuelles (Closed for annual vacation). After this national rest period, business, school, and politics begin again in September.

12. *CAFÉS*

The **café** is one of the best-known symbols of French lifestyle. Open from early till late, serving espresso, drinks, and food before and after restaurants have closed, the **café** is, however, far more than a place to drink. It is a meeting place for students or friends or acquaintances. The casual **"On prend un verre?"** ("Let's have a drink?") can be an invitation to continue an interesting conversation with a new acquaintance, to take a break from grueling work or a boring routine, or to explore the romantic possibilities of a chance encounter.

In the lively and densely populated environment of urban France, where people don't readily invite friends home, the café is the place to meet and talk. It can be somewhere to read, write, or sit on your own over a drink. More importantly, it is a public arena, open to the street (with a glass front in winter and chairs and tables outside in summer), where people can be seen socializing or simply watching the passing crowd. The Paris opening in 2004 of a Starbucks with its take-out coffee in Styrofoam cups produced a clash of cultures with this French café tradition.

The social importance of the **café** is reflected in its ubiquity in every French town or village, even though the number of **cafés** has declined during the last hundred years from over three hundred thousand to forty-three thousand. The visitor to France may notice certain common features. Alcoholic drinks are served in **cafés**. To stand and drink at the counter (**le comptoir** or **le zinc**) costs less than to sit at a table. The hardboiled eggs on the counters are eaten for quick snacks. In old-style **cafés**, the pinball machines (**les flippers**) and the football tables (**les babyfoots**) are played by young and old.

As casual a part of French life as the **café** is, there are established conventions of greeting the waiters and owners. Customers show their formal respect by using the **vous** (formal "you") forms and **Monsieur** and **Madame.** They open an exchange with a **Bonjour, Monsieur/Madame** and say **Au revoir** on leaving. **S'il vous plaît** is used to attract a waiter's attention.

The traditional tip (**le pourboire**) for the waiter has been officially replaced by a service charge included in the bill, but many French customers still leave a small tip as well.

Salons de thé (tearooms) provide a more elegant setting than **cafés**. Originally a fashionable meeting place for women, they have recently increased in number and attracted men as well for a light lunch. They serve nonalcoholic drinks throughout the day and close in the early evening.

13. CALLING CARDS

Calling cards and business cards (both called **cartes de visite**) are frequently used in France. Single and married people send their calling cards, printed with their names and home addresses, instead of commercial greeting cards when issuing invitations and expressing New Year's wishes. The French tradition is to send New Year's greetings, throughout January, rather than Christmas greetings, although Christmas cards appear in shops more often than they used to.

People use a formal style in the messages on their calling cards, which means in part avoiding the use of "I" or "we." An example would be **Monsieur et Madame Jacques Beaumarchais vous souhaitent une très heureuse Nouvelle Année** (Mr. and Mrs. Jacques Beaumarchais wish you a very happy New Year).

Business cards are used much as they are in the United States, although perhaps a little more frequently, in a somewhat wider variety of circumstances, and by a rather wider range of occupations.

Un faire-part is a different sort of card, printed as the occasion demands, to announce births, marriages, and deaths. **Un faire-part** to announce a marriage is sent in the names not only of the parents of the bridal couple but also of all the surviving grandparents. *Le Figaro*, a national daily with a mainly bourgeois readership, prints a special page called **Le Carnet du Jour** (The Daily Notebook) that carries various kinds of **faire-part**.

14. *CHANSON*

In the1960s, young French pop singers introduced a new wave of music called **yéyé** to the generation born after World War II. These young people had become a large group by this time and followed their own styles and tastes, which frequently shocked the conservative older generations. The **yéyé** songs, often adaptations of American and British rock and pop songs, were the first inroads of the international pop culture into France. The name **yéyé** came from the "yeah, yeah" that was heard in songs by the famous British group The Beatles and other American and British groups. The most popular **yéyé** singer was Johnny Hallyday (1943–), whose career evolved from rock to the different styles of pop and who has remained a favorite of the French. As of 2005, he had sold over one hundred million discs and his national concert tours were still filling stadiums.

Pop and rock music has extended its audience through new radio stations like **NRJ**, **Skyrock**, and **Chérie FM** that broadcast continuous music programs for a young audience and have a strong influence on which song will become a hit (**un tube**). A law passed to guarantee French artists an audience and protect French national culture requires that at least 40 percent of the songs a radio station plays must be in French. The French listen to music on average two hours per day. A 2005 survey revealed that 66 percent prefer French singers and 22 percent foreign singers; 29 percent prefer pop and rock music and 22 percent classical music.

The tradition of **la chanson française** (the French song) is uniquely French and not influenced by Anglo-Saxon culture. It is a poetic song, usually written by the singer or a poet, and expresses emotions through evocative lyrics with a simple guitar or piano accompaniment. The **chansons** of Charles Trenet (1913–2001), Georges Brassens (1921–81), Charles Aznavour (1924–), Jacques Brel (1929–78), and Juliette Gréco (1927–) remain popular today, as do the dramatic love songs of Édith Piaf (1915–63). In 2001, 59 percent of discs sold in France were of **la chanson française**. The most recorded song ever is a 1964 song by the **yéyé** and rock singer Claude François called **"Comme d'habitude."** Frank Sinatra turned it into a global success as "My Way."

Francophone singers from Africa, like Youssou N'Dour (Senegal) and Rokai Traoré (Mali), the French-born black singer Pascal Obispo, and numerous French-Canadian singers, among whom Lynda Lamay is a new star, have expanded the horizons of the French song. Accordion music traditionally associated with a baguette-and-beret image of the French and a Paris synonymous with love is attracting new audiences.

In today's world of the globalization of American pop culture, language is a barrier to the international success of French pop singers. However, French electronic music by groups such as Daft Punk and dance music mixed by Parisian DJs and played in discos around the world have taken the "French touch" to many countries.

15. CHIC AND DESIGNER LUXURY GOODS

The French are famous for their sense of elegance and style. Luxury goods have contributed much to the world's traditional image of France. A French origin gives cachet to high-fashion clothes; perfumes carrying the names of leading fashion designers; Hermès silk scarves; Cartier watches and jewelry; Louis Vuitton luggage; Baccarat crystal; vintage wines, like Château Laffite Rothschild and Château d'Yquem; Rémy Martin cognac; and Bollinger, Laurent-Perrier, or Veuve Clicquot champagne. French brands command more than half of the world's luxury goods market.

The French reputation is not underserved. French luxury products benefit from expertise in craft and design accumulated over centuries and place the priority on aesthetic rather than utilitarian principles that the French have maintained. French expertise has not, however, made French markets impregnable to designers of other countries. The pyramid glass entrance to the Louvre Museum, a spectacular and successful combination of the ancient and the modern added in 1989 during bicentenary celebrations of the Revolution, was designed by the Chinese-American architect I. M. Pei (1917–).

16. CINEMA

The Cannes International Film Festival, which began in 1946, attracts international attention in May each year with its **Palme d'Or** (Golden Palm) award for the best film and other awards for the best director and actors. A Festival of American Cinema is held annually in September in Deauville (Normandy).

Paris was the site of the first commercial screening of films. The Lumière brothers, Auguste (1862–1954) and Louis (1864–1948), presented eleven short films, one of which was *La Sortie des usines Lumière* ([Workers] Exiting the Lumière [photographic materials] Factory). The world movie industry originated in the French Pathé studios. In 1908, 70 percent of the American market consisted of French movies.

French cinema has an international reputation, which it has earned particularly for its art films and for its cinema theorists who write for *Les Cahiers du cinéma.* To encourage the production of French movies, the government subsidizes the cinema industry through an 11 percent tax on American movies distributed in France and other taxes. As well as producing the largest number of films in the European Union, France has the highest percentage of moviegoers in Europe. Going to the movies is a very popular pastime, and conversations among friends frequently have recent movies as a topic.

In the French tradition, films are better known for their directors than the actors featured in them. The French director is an author, like a novelist, who makes films in his or her own distinctive style and over which he or she has complete creative control. This contrasts directly with the American Hollywood film tradition, which promotes leading actors rather than directors. The best-known actors from different generations were featured in François Ozon's 2001 movie *8 femmes* (*8 Women*): Danielle Darrieux, Catherine Deneuve, Isabelle Huppert, Fanny Ardant, Firmine Richard, Emmanuelle Béart, Virginie Ledoyen, and Ludivine Ségnier. Gérard Dépardieu (1948–), France's most popular male actor, has appeared in more than 160 films. Famous examples of directors in the French tradition are Jean Renoir (1894–1979); René Clair (1898–1981); and the "New Wave" filmmakers François Truffaut (1932–84), Jean-Luc Godard (1930–), and Claude Chabrol (1930–).

The French movie industry does not imitate the Hollywood-formula blockbuster or musical comedy with spectacular dancing. It prefers psychological and human relationship themes, often involving friendship, love, and infidelity, that are character driven rather than situation driven. French slapstick comedies like the Astérix films and historical dramas are also popular.

French movies made primarily for a French audience have rarely been successful in competing commercially outside France with big-budget Hollywood movies made for an international audience that enjoys action movies. One exception was the 2001 smash hit **Le Fabuleux Destin d'Amélie Poulain** (*Amélie*), directed by Jean-Peirre Jeunet and starring Audrey Tautou playing an offbeat introvert on a mission to spread happiness around Montmartre.

The **Césars**, the French equivalent of the Oscars, celebrated their thirtieth anniversary in 2005. Founded in 1936, the legendary **Ciné-mathèque Française**, which houses France's film library and shows movie classics, is today located in the Bercy district of Paris, in a building designed by the American architect Frank Gehry.

17. *COCORICO!*

The crow of the rooster in France is **cocorico**, not cock-a-doodle-doo as in English. A French dog's bark is **ouah! ouah!** and a French cat's meow is **miaou**.

As the eagle is an emblem of the United States, the rooster (**le coq gaulois**) is an emblem of France. This emblem symbolizes vigilance and arose in the middle of the seventeenth century when an official French medal depicted a rooster chasing away the Spanish lion. France's enemies, in reaction, began to caricature France as a rooster. France adopted the rooster as its official emblem, used on the flagstaff of its army regiments, during the July monarchy (1830–1848) and the Second Republic (1848–52). The seal of the French Republic since 1848 shows the allegorical Liberty seated at a rudder that is decorated with a rooster. French sports teams use the rooster as their emblem in international competitions.

French parodists and cartoonists use **le coq gaulois** and its **cocorico** to lampoon proud French nationalism and chauvinism. If one French person is seen as boasting too much about personal successes, another person in the group is liable to deride the behavior with a **cocorico!**

The rooster on the bell towers of French churches has another history. It represents only the rooster whose crow greets the dawn each day. The militantly secular government of the 1789 Revolution confiscated church property, removed the crosses from the church bell towers that dominated village skylines, and replaced the crosses with roosters.

18. CONVERSATION

The French attach special importance to conversation, which they consider a skill that can be learned and developed to the level of an art. The literary salons of the seventeenth and eighteenth century established the rules of the art. Women of intellect and sophistication presided over the salons, for example, the Marquise de Pompadour (1721–64), King Louis XV's (1710–74) official mistress, in whose salon philosophers and artists gathered to discuss the new theories and ideas of the Age of Enlightenment.

Modern French conversations center on general topics of social and cultural interest and offer the participants an opportunity to exchange ideas and opinions. French people, even in a very relaxed gathering, rarely talk about the weather and even more rarely talk about money or events at work. Food and politics are common topics in what is usually a general discussion in which everyone is expected to voice an opinion. One reason for this is that from an early age, schoolchildren are taught to reason and to analyze a topic from different points of view. Oral examinations are also an important part of their education. This explains the enduring appeal of eloquent expression of ideas at all levels of French society.

An Anglo-Saxon observing French people in conversation is often struck by how they speak out, interrupt each other continually, argue intensely to the point where it seems they will be enemies forever, and then the discussion subsides and everyone is smiling and at ease with each other. Why? Because all of the participants are expected to express their opinions frankly and to defend them when someone disagrees. Intelligent disagreement can be one of the main pleasures of conversation, even between closest friends.

Some foreigners would claim that the French prefer discussion to action. One anonymous Anglo-Saxon businessman, impatient with the delays in acting on a decision because of the French need to discuss its principles, parodied the French attitude as "it sounds all right in practice, but how does it work in theory?" Lengthy discussion of the abstract principles of a project is characteristic of a people whose ideals are intellectual rather than pragmatic.

19. CULTURAL TOURISM

Not all of the visitors who flock to France's museums, galleries, castles, cathedrals, and churches are foreign tourists; many are French themselves. Cultural tourism is very much a part of French education and socialization. Often a family will spend part of its vacation following the itinerary in one of the regional green Michelin guides while a designated family member reads aloud the guide's explanation of the places and buildings of historical and cultural significance. The Michelin guide is something of a cultural icon itself, and reference to it evokes in the French a vision of the bourgeois family vacation. The most popular cultural attractions for French tourists are the Louvre Museum, the Palace of Versailles, the Orsay Museum of Impressionist painters in Paris, the Abbey of St. Michel in Normandy, and the Chambord and Chenonceaux castles in the Loire Valley.

The pleasure the French get from visiting cultural monuments and museums is enhanced by their knowledge of the historical events that have molded their nation and of the characteristics of the art forms in each century. The artifacts and historical events, being a shared cultural experience, serve as examples and points of reference in French conversations and form the basis for the "cultural baggage" that is an important component of being French. The French are very proud of their rich cultural heritage that has built up through the centuries since the time of the prehistoric cave drawings in the southwest region of Périgord and the Roman settlements after Julius Caesar's invasion of Gaul in 52 B.C.

While visiting and admiring their cultural treasures, the French tend to imagine that their civilization is richer than all others, that France is the most civilized of all nations, and that the French way of doing things is the best conceivable way. Many foreigners share the French admiration of the masterpieces of French culture but are critical of the culturally superior attitudes of the French.

20. CULTURE

French governments have always promoted a cultural heritage policy within France as well as actively promoting French language and culture throughout the world. The 1 percent of the national budget allocated to culture is higher than in most countries. The high-culture image of France is generally associated with masterpieces of architecture, painting, sculpture, and music. The Gothic cathedrals, the Impressionist painters, the sculptures by Auguste Rodin (1840–1917) and the music of Hector Berlioz (1803–69) have become icons of international cultural comparison.

French paintings are considered to be an essential component of the leading art museums throughout the world. Art museums in all regions of France exhibit French paintings from the various centuries. In Paris, the main museums are the Louvre, the largest in the world, which displays artworks from antiquity up to 1850; the Orsay Museum, which opened in 1986 and displays works from 1850 to 1914; and the Beaubourg Museum (also called the Georges Pompidou Center), which opened in 1977, for contemporary painting. The Picasso Museum opened in Paris in 1985 to display the paintings, drawings, and sculptures of the Spanish-born Pablo Picasso (1881–1973), arguably the most influential artist of the twentieth century, who did most of his work in France, where he lived from 1904 until his death. The newest museum in Paris is the **Musée des Arts premiers**, which opened in 2006 and was designed by the French architect Jean Nouvel on the Quai Branly on the left bank of the Seine. It exhibits indigenous arts from around the world.

Literature and theater are other forms of high culture that have made France famous around the world by inspiring writers, philosophers, poets, playwrights, and theater directors in many countries.

21. DECORATIONS

A small ribbon or a rosette on the left lapel of a French person's coat is a state award for outstanding civil or military service. A red ribbon or rosette denotes the highest state award, the **Légion d'honneur**, created by Napoleon Bonaparte in 1802, which is accorded particular respect. It and the blue **Ordre national du mérite** are awarded in the name of the president of the Republic.

Each state honor has several grades, designated by the form of the decoration: a ribbon for **chevalier**, the lowest grade; a rosette for **officier**, the next grade; a rosette on a silver **nœud** (knot) for **commandeur**, the highest grade. Some other honors are the mauve **Ordre des palmes académiques**, for service to education, and the green **Ordre des Arts et des Lettres**, for contributions to the arts and literature. French people in these areas of endeavor greatly covet these marks of professional and social rank. The highest award for bravery in military service is the **Croix de guerre**.

22. DOCUMENTS AND FORMS

A French citizen becomes a legal adult and is entitled to vote in national elections at the age of eighteen; from that age, all citizens carry their national identity card (**carte nationale d'identité**), which shows the citizen's name, date of birth, physical characteristics, address, photograph (head shot), and an official stamp. To avoid counterfeiting identity cards, the vital personal information is now recorded on a microchip in the card. Until adulthood, a child's name and date of birth is officially recorded in the **livret de famille** (family booklet), which is issued by city hall.

The national identity card must be carried at all times and produced when requested by the police or by administration officials. Of course, for visitors, passports serve in the place of national identity cards. The cover of the French passport is identical throughout the European Union because the French are both French and European citizens. A **livret du citoyen européen** (European citizen booklet) explaining the rights and duties of European citizens is given to all French people when they turn eighteen and have to attend an obligatory day of "preparation for national defense," which replaced an obligatory period of national military service for young adults.

Other important personal documents are the **carte de sécurité sociale**, granting entitlement to national health benefits, and the **carte d'allocations familiales** (government grants are given to families with children as part of a policy to increase the national birthrate). In addition, all car drivers must have a **permis de conduire** (driver's license) and a **carte grise** with registration details of the car.

The large number and frequent use of these documents in daily life reflects the influence of the state in France. A French citizen goes to the **mairie** (city hall) and other administrative offices when these documents need to be changed and stamped. The civil servants there have a fearsome reputation for applying the letter of the law strictly. The excessive bureaucratic attitudes and large number of forms to be filled out often cause French displays of frustration and annoyance and provide opportunities for the citizenry to exercise their wits by using **le système D**. See **Queues** (Lines).

The identity card and other official documents a French citizen has to carry are called **les papiers** (papers). A police officer performing a security check asks **"Vos papiers, s'il vous plaît!"** ("Your papers, please!) Illegal immigrants are referred to as **les sans-papiers** (without papers).

23. DRINKING

French wines and liqueurs are famous throughout the world. France is the second-largest wine producer; Italy produces more wine, but the French drink more of it. France is the biggest wine exporter in the world. Wine consumption in France has almost halved since the 1960s, when the average consumer drank 100 liters a year. Although that figure has now fallen to 58 liters, it is still the highest in the world. Today there is stricter enforcement of the law against drunk driving, and younger people are increasingly choosing fruit juice, soft drinks, mineral water, or beer instead of wine with their meals. France's Pernod Ricard Company is the third-largest multinational wine and spirits group in world.

The most famous wine-growing regions are Alsace (for white wines), Bordeaux and Burgundy (for both red and white wines), and Beaujolais (for light red wines). On November 17 of each year, the new Beaujolais vintage is successfully promoted around the world with the slogan **Le Beaujolais Nouveau est arrivé** (The new Beaujolais has arrived). Champagne is produced from vineyards between Reims and Épernay, in the northeast of France. The United States is the second largest export market for French wines with champagne constituting 42 percent of that market. Great Britain is the largest export market.

Most French houses and apartment buildings feature a **cave** (cellar) in which bottles of vintage wine are stored for special meals and family celebrations. Wine for daily meals (**vin de table**) can be bought from the supermarket or wine shop.

The French also drink a large quantity of mineral water (**eau minérale**). The Ministry of Health must recognize genuine therapeutic qualities before it will agree to allow a water to be labeled **eau minérale**. **Eau minérale** can be either **gazeuse** (bubbly; Perrier is an international example) or **plate** (still; like Evian). Both water and wine appear on the table at mealtime. French households drink more than twice as much mineral water as wine.

Drinks served at a formal meal follow a set order: before the meal, an **apéritif** (cocktail); white wine with the **hors d'œuvre**, as well as with the main course if it is fish or veal; red wine with a main course of red meat or game and with the cheese; champagne with the cake or dessert if the meal is a celebration; and a **digestif** (liqueur) such as cognac or a fruit liqueur after coffee.

In addition to champagne on special occasions, popular **apéritifs** are **kir** (named after a Dijon priest who was a hero in the Résistance), made by mixing black currant liqueur (**cassis**) with white wine—or with champagne, in which case it is **un kir royal**; **pastis**, an aniseed-flavored spirit that is popular in the South, especially in summer; and red martini or port wine (**porto**) served with ice.

Usually only coworkers will drink wine together in a **café**. Friends from other social groups meeting for a drink will order a coffee, a beer, or fruit juice. Today Coca-Cola (**un Coca**) is popular among French teenagers.

The north and east of France, which border beer-drinking Germany, Belgium, and Holland, have a beer-drinking tradition and produce two popular brands of French beer, Kronenbourg and Kanterbrau. France in general is only the seventh largest in beer consumption in Europe, with the average consumer drinking thirty-seven liters of beer per year. British-style pubs serving many types of beer are now common throughout France. It was a Frenchman, Louis Pasteur (1822–95), who in 1873 successfully devised a method to kill disease-producing organisms in beer by raising the temperature in the brewing process.

24. DRIVING

Renault, Peugeot, and Citroën are cars of French design that are exported to many countries. In 2004, more than a quarter of the cars manufactured by Renault and the Peugeot-Citroën group were sold outside Western Europe. The Renault Company, founded in 1899 by Louis Renault (1877–1944), was nationalized in 1945. In 1998, the Renault Company took effective control of the Japanese company Nissan, and, in 2005, the combined Renault-Nissan group was the third-largest car manufacturer in the world.

More than half of French drivers own a French-made car. Import quotas limit the number of Japanese cars on French roads. Every two years in October, the Paris Motor Show, **Mondial de l'Automobile**, attracts huge crowds.

An extensive network of **autoroutes** (national superhighways) covers France. A great many are toll roads (**autoroutes à péage**). Traffic on the **autoroutes** is very heavy at the beginning and end of weekends and during the summer vacation months of July and August. Drivers sometimes use the national roads (**routes nationales**) to avoid paying tolls.

A common French motoring expression is **conduire comme un fou** (to drive like a madman). Dealing with other drivers brings out the impatient, aggressive, and argumentative side of the French nature. French individualism has not encouraged an ethic of considerateness for other drivers. Honking insultingly, gesturing, and screaming abuse at other drivers is frequent. The last two numbers on car plates indicate the **département** (administrative district) where the car was registered. A "75" indicates that the car was registered in Paris, and drivers of these cars are particularly notorious for their aggressive driving.

French drivers dislike paying for parking in underground lots (**parkings**); in congested Paris, they often leave their cars parked on the sidewalk or across building entrances. The Parisian driving experience provides further challenges because of the trucks and cars double-parked for deliveries or for shopping on the way home. Abuse of parking regulations and failure to pay parking fines is not discouraged by the genial practice of general amnesty of French parking tickets at the installation of each new president of the Republic.

Speeding, driving after drinking too much, and the common practice of tailgating were the main causes of the deaths of 7,242 people on the roads in 2002. That year, President Chirac in his 14 July national speech declared that such a high number of road fatalities "is unworthy of a great modern country." Since then, increased use of radar to catch speeding drivers, automatic penalties, and harsher sentences for traffic offenses, including drunk driving, have dramatically decreased the number of fatal road accidents, which fell by 21 percent from 2002 to 2003.

Huge crowds of car-racing enthusiasts are attracted to the Formula One Monte Carlo Rally, to the **24 heures du Mans** (a twenty-four-hour car race at Le Mans in western France), and to the rally from Paris to Dakar (the capital of Senegal in Africa).

25. ECOLOGY

France protects the flora, fauna, and ecological environment in the large state national parks, principally in the mountain regions of the **Alpes**, the **Pyrénées**, the **Cévennes**, and in the **Camargue** on the Mediterranean coast. Marine life and the ecology of small islands are protected in underwater national parks around the French Mediterranean and Corsica. Jacques Cousteau (1910–1997), the famous underwater explorer, was a leading French environmentalist.

The Green movement did not develop a social base in France until the late 1980s. It grew out of the Student Revolt of May 1968 as a protest movement, but the 1974 oil crisis and the resulting economic crisis of the late 1970s and 1980s relegated the movement to a minor role in the French political dialogue. Part of the government's response to France's energy crisis and lack of oil and other natural energy resources was to develop nuclear energy, and the strategy enjoyed wide public support, further weakening the Green movement's appeal. France gets more than 80 percent of its electricity from nuclear power.

Several events in the later 1980s galvanized French concern over environmental issues, and French attitudes shifted dramatically. In 1986, the Chernobyl nuclear reactor disaster threatened all Europe with nuclear fallout. French news media, like news media around the world, focused attention on the gap in the ozone layer, the greenhouse effect, acid rain, and the destruction of the Amazon rain forest. A number of oil tanker accidents polluted stretches of the French coastline.

The Green political party (**les Verts**) polled almost 7 percent of votes in the parliamentary elections in 1997. It joined with the Socialist and

Communist parties to form **la gauche plurielle** (the pluralist left) that governed France from 1997 to 2002. The Socialist leader Lionel Jospin was prime minister and the leader of **les Verts**, a woman, Dominique Voynet, was minister for the environment. A coalition of conservative parties swept this government from power in the 2002 elections. Since then, the Green movement has split into quarreling factions and has lost its high profile.

In 2004, President Chirac proposed an Environment Charter that would enshrine the right of all French people to "live in an environment that is balanced and respects their health." France was among the first countries to sign the international Kyoto Protocol, which was implemented in 2005 to reduce global warming by limiting carbon dioxide emissions.

26. EDUCATION

French parents have a constant preoccupation with the education of their children. Children who achieve top grades in France's national education system, which is based on intellectual merit without concern for wealth or privilege, can expect the financial and social rewards of a brilliant career. In principle, intellectually gifted children from the French working class benefit from this democratic principle and can graduate with similar career and social rewards. In reality, the success rate of children from the wealthy bourgeoisie is higher.

The French education system is national and highly centralized. The state education system is based on three fundamental principles. It is **obligatoire** (compulsory) for all children until the age of sixteen; it is **gratuit** (free); and it is **laïc** (secular). The principle of **laïcité** (secularism) was enforced when a law was passed in 2004 banning the wearing in state schools of ostensibly religious symbols (particularly the wearing of headscarves by Muslim girls).

Primary and secondary schools are administered nationally, which means that course content is the same for all subjects and national examinations are the same for all students. The state subsidizes private (mostly religious) schools, which make up 14 percent of primary schools and 21 percent of secondary schools and are attended by 20 percent of the school population. The subsidies are still controversial in republican France.

French pupils become accustomed to long hours at school and lots of homework from an early age. Primary school classes start between 8 and 8:30 A.M., there is a two-hour break for lunch, and classes end after 4:30. Children then come home, have a snack, and do their homework, which is often supervised by their mothers, before having dinner at 7:00 P.M. or later.

Students in their final high school year (at around the age of eighteen) sit for the **baccalauréat** or **bac**. They are under pressure to achieve good grades on this national exam because its results determine their future study and career possibilities. A perfect score on the **bac** is 20; students who score above 10 are entitled to enroll in one of the universities, all of which are state financed. Because of the tremendous number of students enrolled in first-year university classes, students must learn to work independently. They receive far less guidance and personal assistance from their instructors than American students. Most assessment is done by intellectually demanding formal exams that a large proportion of students fail; as a result, many discontinue their university studies.

Students spend the first four years of their high school studies at a **collège** and the last three years of their high school studies at a **lycée**. Those who have the best academic performance during their **lycée** studies and at the **baccalauréat** may apply to enroll in a two-year preparatory class for one of the entrance examinations to the **Grandes Écoles** instead of enrolling at university. There are about a hundred **Grandes Écoles**, also state financed, whose purpose is to prepare students for specific professions. Only the best students pass the barrier of the competitive entrance examinations to these **Écoles**, whose diplomas in many cases are a virtual guarantee of a high-ranking position in a particular profession. In such a hierarchical system, parents' obsession with their children's scholastic performance in primary and secondary school is understandable, as is their reverence for the most prestigious **Grandes Écoles: l'École Polytechnique** (see X), **l'École Nationale d'Administration (ENA)**, and **l'École des Hautes Études Commerciales (HEC)**.

All attempts to reform this rigid educational system provoke heated controversy from parents, who want their children to benefit from its hierarchical structure, and from secondary and university students, who are quick to organize street demonstrations. Ever since the successful student demonstrations that fueled the national strike by workers and the public revolt in May 1968, mass student demonstrations have usually succeeded in forcing the government to withdraw the proposed reforms. Two recent examples of successful demonstrations are noteworthy. An attempt to impose entrance quotas to universities brought students into the streets to defend the right of all students with a **baccalauréat** to enroll for university studies. In 2005, a proposed reform of awarding the **baccalauréat** to include a component of continuous assessment sparked huge national demonstrations by high school students.

27. EUROPE

Two Frenchmen, Robert Schuman (1886–1963) and Jean Monnet (1888–1979) are called the founders of modern Europe. They envisioned an organization to promote cooperation between European countries, thus ensuring lasting peace between Germany and France after two devastating world wars. Schuman proposed the European Coal and Steel Community (the first United Europe project, ratified in 1951). Despite their traditional rivalry, France and Germany took the initiative in constructing the European Union. The European Union has added some terms of Euro-jargon to French vocabulary: **Eurocrate**, **Europhile**, **Eurosceptique**, **Eurocentrique**, and **Europol** (the police force).

Six countries (Belgium, France, Germany, Italy, Luxembourg, and the Netherlands) signed the Rome Treaty of 1957 to create the European

Economic Community (EEC, popularly called the Common Market). The goal was to create a customs union between the six countries, allowing the free circulation of capital, goods, and people, and to implement common policies regarding agriculture, trade, energy, and transportation. Denmark, Ireland, and the United Kingdom became members in 1973; Greece joined in 1981 and Portugal and Spain in 1986. In 1992, these twelve countries signed the Maastricht Treaty and established the European Union (E.U.), which, with no trade barriers between member countries, formed a powerful economic bloc. Austria, Finland, and Sweden joined in 1995. The number of countries in the European Union increased from fifteen to twenty-five in 2004 when Cyprus, the Czech Republic, Estonia, Hungary, Latvia, Lithuania, Malta, Poland, Slovakia, and Slovenia became members. The E.U. population was then 456 million, and there were twenty official languages.

The economic unification of the European Union has been very successful, aided by the European Central Bank created by the Maastricht Treaty. In 2002, twelve of the member countries (Austria, Belgium, Finland, France, Germany, Greece, Ireland, Italy, Luxembourg, the Netherlands, Portugal, and Spain) adopted a common currency, the euro. The euro area represents the second-largest economy and financial market after the United States, and the euro is the second most important currency in the world's financial markets. The European Union is the world's largest trading bloc and the world's largest exporter of merchandise goods and services.

Less successful has been the development of a unified E.U. foreign policy, despite the formation of a European army. Member countries had conflicting reactions to the invasion of Kuwait by Iraq in 1992, to the wars between the republics of the former Yugoslavia that began in 1993, and to the American-led invasion of Iraq in 2003. E.U. members have, however, been unified in supporting the Kyoto Protocol limiting carbon dioxide emissions to address the disastrous effects of global warming on the environment.

The main decision-making body of the European Union is the European Council, consisting of the twenty-five heads of state and government. The European Commission, located in Brussels (Belgium) administers the European Union.

The European Parliament is located in Strasbourg (France), where it meets monthly. Extraordinary sessions and meetings of its committees take place in Brussels. Its members are elected for five-year terms in national elections; its first president was a Frenchwoman, Simone Veil (1927–). Each country has a number of seats corresponding to its size of population.

The parliament's powers were mostly advisory until the Maastricht Treaty gave it power to approve the European Commission's budget and amend its decisions, block agreements with outside countries, and veto appointments to the E.U. executive agencies. These changes were aimed at giving the elected body representing the European citizens more control over the European Commission bureaucracy and involving them more closely in the functioning of European democracy.

After Germany, the population of France is the largest in the European Union. Within France, there has been a deep division between those who supported closer integration of member countries and those who, fearing a loss of French identity and objecting to the influence on their lives from decisions made by European institutions, wanted a more independent France within Europe. When Charles de Gaulle (1890–1970) was president from 1958 to 1969, he wanted only a loose association of independent nations and opposed any suggestion of a supranational entity or identity. French presidents since 1969 have been more in favor of European integration. However, at the referendum held in France in 1992 to ratify the signing of the Maastricht Treaty, the "yes" vote polled only 51 percent. The French economy has become increasingly integrated with the E.U. economy. The French carry European passports and their lives are increasingly influenced by the decisions of the E.U. institutions.

The functioning of the European Union with twenty-five member countries is much more complex than when there were fifteen members. To streamline the decision-making process in the expanded European Union, a Constitution defining a new distribution of the powers and roles between the member countries and the E.U. institutions was drawn up. This Constitution was to strengthen the political unification of the European Union by an elected president of the Council, by creating the position of minister for foreign affairs and European security, and by increasing the powers of the European Parliament. All member countries had to ratify the Constitution before it took effect. A referendum held in France in May 2005 to ratify the Constitution lost, as did a similar referendum in the Netherlands in June.

The anti–European Union feeling, evident in France's rejection of the proposed Constitution, was confirmed in a **Sofres** opinion poll in September 2005. No longer does a majority of French people agree with all the presidents of the Fifth Republic, who proposed Europe as **"l'avenir de la France"** (the future of France) and the door to economic development and modernization after the loss of the French colonial empire. In the poll, Europe is associated with the idea of "freedom to travel, study, and work everywhere in Europe" for 52 percent of the French; of "peace" for 46 percent; and of "cultural diversity" for 53 percent. However, Europe is synonymous with "democracy," "economic prosperity," and "social protection" for only 24 percent, 17 percent, and 15 percent respectively. In answer to the question of whether belonging to Europe makes France prosperous, 29 percent answered "more prosperous" and 43 percent answered "less prosperous." Forty-one percent (58 percent of workers) consider they are living "less well" because of Europe, only 22 percent consider they are "living better," and 33 percent neither "better or worse." For the necessary changes to be made to the present institutional framework so that the European Union can function more efficiently with twenty-five member countries, French political leaders face a huge challenge to restore confidence in the construction of Europe.

28. *EXTRA!*

The English and French languages have both borrowed the Latin word *extra*. Like many French words that resemble English words, the French meaning is different. A French teenager who says **"Cette glace est extra!"** does not mean that the ice cream costs more, but that it is fantastic. **Extra** in French is a colloquial shortening of **extraordinaire** (extraordinary).

Some other false friends of English speakers in French are **le foot** (soccer), **le car** (tour bus), **la location** (hiring or renting), and **sensible** (sensitive). The real words for *foot, car, location,* and *sensible* are **le pied, la voiture, l'endroit,** and **raisonnable.** Some borrowed English words have an associated meaning like **un camping** (a camping site) and **un parking** (a parking lot).

29. FAMILY

The family unit is extremely important at all levels of French society. Attitudes toward marriage and divorce have changed significantly in recent years, but the family remains the nucleus of daily and social life. In a 2003 survey asking French people what is most important for them, 48 percent answered "the family," 7 percent answered "perfect love," and 7 percent "sincere friendship." In another survey, 88 percent of women said that having children is essential for their happiness.

The traditional concept of the family as a married couple with children has evolved considerably since the 1970s. The proportion of single-parent families increased from 3 percent in 1975 to 7.2 percent in 2000. Because their parents have divorced or separated, 12 percent of children live usually with their mother. Eleven percent of children live in families in which at least one of the parents has remarried. Forty-seven percent of first children are born to unmarried parents. As a result, the family environment has changed. Greater equality between parents and greater autonomy for the children have replaced the authoritarian role of the traditional father. The extended family made up of blood relatives has shrunk (twenty-four extended family members is today's average, but, for 10 percent of the population, the average is less than nine). This is why today's extended family sometimes includes close family friends.

After declining in the 1990s, the birthrate has risen again and France had the highest birthrate in Europe in 2003. The government gives generous family allowances to encourage couples to have more children. Two children per family has become the average. Families with a large number of children have become the exception. There are four children in 13 percent of families and six children in 3 percent of them. In families where at least one parent is an immigrant, the average number of children is higher, and 15 percent of all French births are in such families.

Mealtimes play an essential role in maintaining the nuclear family unit. Children are expected to sit at the table and have their meals with their parents. This is one of the many forms of disciplined socialization that results in French children behaving like adults from an early age and having a strong sense of belonging to a family. The extended family gathers on many occasions to celebrate family events with a special meal. The extended network of relatives provides valuable social and career support as children move through adolescence and begin to enter the workforce.

Grandparents are increasingly giving financial assistance to their children and grandchildren who have lost their jobs or have been unable to get a first job during the decades of high unemployment. At age sixteen, 95 percent of French children live with their parents; at age twenty, 60 percent of males and 45 percent of females do. When children do leave home, they tend to live fairly close to their parents, and vacations usually include time with the extended family.

30. FASHION

Each year in January and August, Paris's **grands couturiers** (leading fashion designers) present their new collections. The spectacular shows on their catwalks attract the fashion writers and photographers for the huge readership of women's magazines across the world, and Paris reasserts its position as the fashion capital of the world. On the streets of the city, French style means dressing smartly, with attitude.

The founder of modern fashion was Charles Worth (1825–95), an Englishman who settled in Paris in 1845 and established the first **mai-**

son de haute couture (high-fashion house) there in 1858. His dress designs, using the highest-quality materials and workmanship, dictated women's fashions at the court of Emperor Napoleon III (1808–73), and the other courts of Europe imitated them.

The designs of Paul Poiret (1879–1944) and Coco Chanel (1883–1971) set the fashion for a more flowing, comfortable style, freeing women from corsets. Chanel pioneered the use of jersey, a supple fabric, and the wearing of costume jewelry.

Paris's reputation was enhanced when leading designers opened numerous **maisons de haute couture** there: Jean Patou (1880–1936), Madeleine Vionnet (1876–1975), and Jeanne Lanvin (1867–1946).

Christian Dior (1905–57) launched the New Look in 1947, after years of austerity and deprivation during World War II, and reestablished Paris as the trendsetter. Pierre Cardin (1922–) and Yves Saint-Laurent (1936–) continued Dior's success; their new fashion silhouettes were copied worldwide. More recent trendsetters have been Christian Lacroix (1952–) and Jean-Paul Gaultier (1952–), who was chosen by Madonna to design her stage costumes. In the late 1990s, two young British designers, John Galliano (1960–), who heads the house of Christian Dior, and Alexander McQueen (1969–), brought a new burst of sexy, creative energy to the Paris catwalks. Designers also market their own labels of prestige perfumes that have become as famous as their fashions.

All contemporary designers create collections of ready-to-wear clothes (**prêt-à-porter**) and accessories as well as exclusive **maisons de haute couture** gowns, a nod to the changing lifestyles and budgets of modern career women. The main French **maisons de haute couture** are owned by two French conglomerates: LVMH (Louis Vuitton Moët Hennessy), whose CEO Bernard Arnault, the richest man in France, devised the new international appeal of French luxury brands, and PPR (Pinault, Printemps, Redoute), which includes La Redoute (the highly successful mail-order company), whose CEO François Pinault owns the most extensive contemporary art collection in France.

31. FLOWERS AND GARDENS

In France, as in many countries, red roses are a symbol of love and beauty. They also became the symbol of the French Socialist Party when François Mitterrand (1916–1996) was elected president in 1981. Chrysanthemums are not given as a present because they are traditionally placed on family graves in visits on **Toussaint** (All Saints' Day) on 1 November. A flower is also associated with the Labor Day holiday (**la fête du Travail**); lily-of-the-valley (**le muguet**) is given to friends and family on that day to bring them happiness (**un porte-bonheur**). The French spend on average 32€ each year to buy bouquets of flowers, the favorites being roses, gladioli, and orchids.

The French style of garden (**jardin à la française**) is geometrical, with frequent use of ponds, fountains, and statues; the landscape architect André Le Nôtre (1613–1700), who designed the gardens of the Palace of Versailles, originated it. The Tuileries Gardens near the Louvre and the Luxembourg Gardens near the Sorbonne, both in Paris, are examples of the style. In public gardens, a frequent sign is **Pelouse interdite**, indicating that walking and sitting on the grass is forbidden.

The Impressionist painter Claude Monet's (1840–1926) garden at Giverny in Normandy, where he painted his radiant "Water Lilies" (**"Nymphéas"**) series from 1899 to his death, and which has been maintained with the help of American philanthropists, attracts crowds of admiring visitors. The annual Summer International Garden Festival at the castle of Chaumont-sur-Loire, in the center of France, is also extremely popular.

32. *FRANCOPHONIE*

French is spoken across all the world continents and is, after English, the most spoken world language. It is estimated that there are 175 million

French speakers. French is the official language of twenty-nine countries and the major language of another twelve countries. Accents and vocabulary in **Québec**, **Haïti**, and **Sénégal**, for example, vary greatly from one another and from what one hears in France, such as **"jasette"** in **Québec** for **"causette"** (chat). In the Caribbean **DOM** (overseas departments; see Overseas Departments and Territories) and **la Réunion**, French Creole is the everyday language. This diversity is a source of vitality for the continuing universal use of French.

Francophonie is the term used to describe the world community of countries in which French is the national language or is used for official or administrative purposes. Since 1986, a **Sommet de la Francophonie** brings together every two years the heads of state or government of countries that "share the French language" to promote a dialogue between cultures and between developed and developing countries. In 2004, the tenth **Sommet** was held in Ouagadougou in the African country of Burkina-Faso.

The former president of **Sénégal**, Abdou Diouf, is the Secretary General of the International Organization of Francophonie, which is made up of fifty-one member countries and five countries with observer status. The latest country to join is Greece, "to help protect itself from domination by a single language (English)." The French government allocates $1 billion annually to promote French internationally. The International Day of Francophonie has been celebrated on 20 March every year since 1988.

Although French is an official working language at the United Nations and in the administration of the European Union, its use in these international institutions is declining. French remains the primary language at international institutions like UNESCO, Interpol, and the European Court of Justice. French has the same status as English in all official announcements at the Olympic Games (**les Jeux Olympiques**), which were relaunched in 1894 by the Frenchman Pierre de Coubertin. The Fifth **Jeux de la Francophonie** for francophone athletes took place in the **Niger** capital of Niamey in 2005.

33. FRIENDSHIP

The French make a clear distinction between friends (**amis, amies**) and acquaintances (**connaissances**). Foreigners have often observed that it is not easy to progress beyond acquaintance and become accepted as a friend in France. A casual relationship develops into friendship only after a considerable amount of time. The French usually have only a small number of close friends (**proches** or **grands amis, grandes amies**) in addition to their immediate family, and they tend to belong to the same social background. Family and close friends form a group of **proches** who see each other regularly for a meal or a drink and during vacations. Their friendship lasts throughout their lives.

Patterns of friendship are changing as today's young generation travels more, becomes more outward-looking, and adopts a more relaxed approach to life. Students use the **tu** (informal *you*) form automatically with each other instead of the **vous** (formal *you*) form, which is traditionally used when people meet for the first time. Shared interests and intellectual affinities are increasingly the reason for becoming friends. Such friendships cut across social barriers, which previously limited the possibilities of making close friends outside one's social group.

34. FROGS AND SNAILS, GARLIC AND TRUFFLES

An old British cliché parodies the French as a bizarre people who constantly eat frogs (**grenouilles**), snails (**escargots**), garlic (**ail**), and tree-root fungi such as truffles (**truffes**)—a disgusting diet to the traditional British palate accustomed to plain food and fish and chips. The cliché gave rise to the popular British name for the French, the "Frogs."

This national cliché is as exaggerated as all national clichés are. These food items are relatively uncommon on French menus, with the exception of garlic, which figures in many dishes as it does in all Mediterranean cuisines. Some restaurants offer frogs' legs and Burgundy snails as appetizers before the main course. Pigs and dogs are trained to find black truffles, a rare and expensive delicacy that grows symbiotically on hazelnut roots in the south of France. The French Christmas meal traditionally begins with a tiny piece of truffle on another delicacy, **foie gras** (the enlarged livers of geese that have been force fed). (See Christmas.)

So much of French life involves eating and culinary traditions that countries that give little importance to fine food satirize the French as obsessive about their stomachs and make fun of what they select from nature to put on their plates. (See Gastronomy and Restaurants.)

35. GAMBLING

Napoleon Bonaparte (1769–1821) outlawed gambling for money, and it has been illegal continuously since—except, of course, for state-run gambling activities, which are run by **La Française des Jeux** and **Le Pari mutuel urbain** (**PMU**).

More than 50 percent of the French population does some gambling, hoping that their luck will win them some money and perhaps a fortune. People buy tickets in **Loto** (created in 1976) and **Rapido** or scratch lottery tickets (like instant lotteries) such as **Millionnaire, Banco,** or **Tac-Otac**. In addition, more than two million French people gamble each week on a European Loto, **Euro Millions**, launched in 2004.

The **PMU** controls off-course betting on horse racing. The tradition of bettors lining up in **cafés** on Sunday mornings to place their bets began to change in 2003 with the introduction of **PMU** Internet betting. The launch of betting places called **Pariez Spot** has also increased the popularity of the **PMU**. Bets are placed on **le tiercé** (choosing first through third place correctly), **le quarté** (chosing first through fourth place correctly), or **le quinté** (choosing first through fifth place correctly). Thirty-three percent of **PMU** gamblers are under thirty-five years of age, and 40 percent are women.

The state also receives income from gambling casinos. These casinos are usually in seaside resorts like Deauville (on the Normandy coast) and Cannes (on the Mediterranean), in lakeside resorts like Annecy (in the Alps), and in spa towns like Vichy (in the center of France).

36. GASTRONOMY AND RESTAURANTS

French cuisine is famous around the world, and the French themselves are famous for their enjoyment of fine food. A constant reason that tourists give for visiting France is to eat French food and go to a French restaurant. The authoritative Michelin guide classifies top French restaurants as three-, two-, and one-star. A chef at a restaurant that achieves three stars becomes internationally famous by that very fact. In 2004, only twenty-seven restaurants were awarded three stars.

The high standards of French chefs did not begin in this century. Vatel, the principal chef of the Prince de Condé (1621–86), killed himself with his own sword in 1671 because the seafood had not arrived in time for a dinner the prince was giving in honor of King Louis XIV (1638–1715). The story goes that it was Marie de Médicis (1573–1642)— and the Italian chefs she brought to France with her as a safeguard against the uncertain quality of food preparation in her adopted country—who began the French tradition of fine cooking.

French culinary traditions have been popularized internationally by famous chefs such as Marie-Antoine Carême (1784–1833); Auguste Escoffier (1846–1935), whose *Guide Culinaire* (1920) is still used today by cooks in every country; and Paul Bocuse (1926–), whose international television programs added a new dimension to the French bourgeois style of cooking by the use of fresh seasonal market produce.

In the early 1980s, chef Michel Olivier (1932–) introduced a new style of cooking called **nouvelle cuisine** or **cuisine minceur** (slim cooking), which spread to fine restaurants everywhere and influenced new Californian cuisine. **Nouvelle cuisine** eliminated excessive butter and fats from traditional French sauces and recipes and highlighted lightness, simplicity, and the artistic presentation of small portions of food on the diner's plate.

Leading chefs of today, such as Joël Robuchon (1945–) and Alain Ducasse (1956–), who was the first chef to have two restaurants awarded three stars, have moved beyond classic French cooking. A recent innovation is fusion cuisine combining French and Asian flavors or using uncommon ingredients and spices from around the world in French regional dishes. There has also been renewed popularity for simple family recipes used by grandmothers. French cooking expressions are used internationally, and French dishes appear on restaurant menus all over the world.

France is an agriculturally rich country, and the diversity of market produce in its regions has created lasting regional food traditions. **Choucroute garnie** in Alsace, **crêpes** in Brittany, **cassoulet** in the southwest, **bouillabaisse** along the Mediterranean coast, and **couscous** from Algeria and former North African colonies are well known. Towns and provinces have become bywords by virtue of their best-known food products and found permanent places in French gastronomic tradition: Dijon mustard, the Champagne province's sparkling wine, Bordeaux red wines, the brandy of Cognac, Bresse chicken, and Roquefort cheese are only a few examples. There are so many regional cheeses that Charles de Gaulle (1890–1970) could invoke this diversity as a symbol of French individualism: **"Un pays qui compte 350 sortes de fromage, c'est ingouvernable"** ("A country with 350 kinds of cheese is ungovernable").

American-inspired fast-food restaurants (**la restauration rapide**) are now everywhere in France, and sales of frozen foods have increased. The modern working woman has less time for elaborate recipes. All the same, the French cook still seeks out the best suppliers of fresh produce in the street markets, and the French list eating as their principal source of pleasure. The seasonal arrival of asparagus, cantaloupes, peaches, and strawberries is a gastronomic event that occasions celebration and conversation at the family dining table.

Concerns about the excessive use of chemicals by farmers in raising cattle or crop production were highlighted by an outbreak of mad cow disease (**la vache folle**). Organic food (**la nourriture bio**) is increasingly popular, as are light-food brands (**les produits allégés**) containing less sugar, fat, and salt. Strong and sometimes even violent oppposition to genetically modified crops, led by José Bové (1953–) and his Farmers' Union, has caused the French government to place a ban on them until there is firm scientific proof that GM foods (**les OGM**) have no harmful effects.

The French playwright Molière (1622–73) wrote **"Il faut manger pour vivre et ne pas vivre pour manger"** ("You must eat to live and not live to eat"). French people today typically paraphrase his words in reverse to express personal and national satisfaction in their gastronomic traditions. The festive atmosphere produced by delicious food, wine, and animated conversation expresses the conviviality for which the French are justly famous. As the gastronome Brillat Savarin (1755–1826) wrote, **"Un bon repas favorise la conversation; un bon vin lui donne de l'esprit"** ("A good meal encourages conversation; a good wine makes it spirited").

37. GENDARMES AND DEMONSTRATIONS

The police officers charged with traffic control and security outside cities are called **gendarmes**, and they are based at the local **gendarmerie** (a branch of the French army). In cities, police officers are **agents de police**, based at the local **commissariat de police** (police station). Their mission is the usual range of law and order enforcement and traffic control, as well as the administrative supervision of foreign and immigrant residents.

The revolutionary tradition in France, that began when the 1789 Revolution led to the creation of the First Republic, continues to have a strong influence on public life. France has a history of large, politically motivated street demonstrations (**manifestations,** or **manifs**), in which people of all ages and from all walks of life take part if they feel strongly on the subject. Vanloads of police parked on the side streets supervise **manifs** vigilantly, and the **CRS** (**Compagnies Républicaines de Sécurité**; the riot police) will be on hand if passions seem likely to run high.

This strong culture of street protests is maintained by political parties and trade unions demonstrating against government plans to change enshrined workers' rights and by agricultural unions demonstrating against European Union policies that would reduce the income of French farmers and winegrowers. Since the May revolt in 1968, every attempt by the government to introduce school and university reform has resulted in massive street demonstrations by students, teachers, and parents. Demonstrations are often the occasion for workers on strike for specific professional reasons and other social groups to air their grievances publicly.

The police are authorized to conduct random identity checks (**contrôles d'identité**) by asking for the national identity card in the street or in metro or train stations. The police usually concentrate such efforts on people of African or North African appearance because of concerns about illegal immigration (**immigration clandestine**).

38. GESTURES

Italians are often parodied for their dramatic gestures when they speak. The French, especially southerners, also gesture a lot. Even naturally undemonstrative French people often speak with their hands and use facial expressions and bodily gestures to add force or nuance to the spoken word.

Americans and, to a lesser degree, the British are socially trained to smile a lot; the French are not. In fact, when asked for an opinion, their first reaction is frequently to pout their lips (**faire une moue**) and shrug their shoulders. Foreigners who are not used to this reaction may incorrectly interpret this French pouting as a sign of rudeness or contempt for people from other countries.

Almost no gesture is universal, but some gestures are at least multinational. The American gesture for "crazy," circling the index finger near the temple, closely resembles the French gesture with the same meaning (**"dingue"**), pointing the index finger at the temple and twisting the hand back and forth. The English expression "My foot!" translates into French as **"Mon oeil!"** ("My eye!"), and the French expression has a convenient gesture that can accompany or replace it—pulling the lower eyelid down slightly with the index finger. This gesture is also a convenient and quick way of indicating to other listeners that you don't believe the speaker's version of events.

Several parts of the body may coordinate in French gestures. To say "I don't know" or "Beats me" (**"Je ne sais pas,"** or **"J'sais pas"**), a French person can pout lips, raise eyebrows, push his or her head forward slightly, raise shoulders, and raise the hands to shoulder level with palms out and upward.

French start counting from the thumb, not the index finger. Since the thumb and index finger equal two, an American ordering two beers in France with the index and middle fingers might well receive three, however much the thumb was curled out of sight.

Americans tend to hear only what is said. French pay attention to how something is said and what is left unsaid. French tend to stand or lean closer to each other in conversation than Americans do. Two French speakers standing close, leaning toward each other, and employing the standard set of pouts, shrugs, and hand gestures gives an American observer the impression that the two are speaking intensely and reacting with animated emotion. It is wise to remember that this is style and habit and not to be misled into drawing psychological conclusions about the speakers or the national temperament from such observations. The two could just be having a simple conversation.

39. GOVERNMENT AND POLITICS

France is a republic, and the majority of French people take great pride in their country's history and place in the world. Since the Declaration of the Rights of Man and of the Citizen in 1789, **la République** has known many ups and downs. France is currently in its Fifth Republic, which was founded in 1958 by Charles de Gaulle (1890–1970). It is a presidential regime in which voters elect their president for a five-year term (since 2002) in a national direct vote, elect members of a National Assembly (**L'Assemblée nationale**) for five-year terms, and vote at other times for councils of their **région** and locality and for French representatives in the European Parliament. Members of the Senate (**Le Sénat**) are elected for nine years, some by direct vote and others by an electoral college.

The presidents of the Fifth Republic have been General Charles de Gaulle (1959–69); Georges Pompidou (1969–74); Valéry Giscard d'Estaing (1974–81); François Mitterrand, the first Socialist politician to be president (1981–95); and Jacques Chirac (1995–2007). As head of state, the president has considerable powers in addition to responsibility for foreign policy and defense but is expected to leave the day-to-day running of the country to the prime minister and his or her government.

The prime minister is selected by the president from the majority party in the National Assembly. The prime minister then appoints a government (a set of ministers) with the president's approval and runs the country according to the Assembly majority's political program. The members of the government don't have to be elected members of the National Assembly or even belong to the prime minister's party. When the president and the prime minister are from different political parties, they must agree to cooperate according to the functions of their office as defined in the Constitution. This arrangement is called **cohabitation**. **Cohabitation** occurred twice during the Socialist François Mitterrand's presidency when there was a conservative prime minister (Jacques

Chirac from 1986 to 1988 and Édouard Balladur from 1993 to 1995) and during Jacques Chirac's presidency when the Socialist Lionel Jospin was prime minister from 1997 to 2002. Local politics remain extremely important in France. Councilors (**conseillers**) elected by the residents of **régions** (regions), **départements** (administrative districts), and **communes** (municipalities) hold power under the reform legislation of the 1980s that decentralized administration in France. The smallest administrative unit is the **commune**, of which there are thirty-six thousand in France. Each commune has a mayor (**maire**), elected by the members of the municipal council.

French political parties have traditionally been split between **la droite**, the conservative right, and **la gauche**, the Socialist, Communist, and Green left. Founded in 1972 by Jean-Marie Le Pen, the **Front National**, an extreme right-wing party, progressively attracted support for its anti-immigration policy during the following decades of increasing unemployment and for its populist opposition to France's integration into the European Union. In the first round of the presidential elections in 2002, Jean-Marie Le Pen, the National Front's candidate, won the second-largest percentage of votes (17 percent) after Jacques Chirac (20 percent), the conservative party's candidate, who was standing for reelection as president. The Socialist candidate, the previous prime minister, Lionel Jospin, was third. In the second round, when voters choose between the two candidates who won the highest number of votes in the first round, Jacques Chirac, with the support of the left-wing parties, was elected with 82 percent of the vote. After the election, the left-wing parties resumed their ideological opposition to a conservative president. In the regional council elections three years later, the Socialists won in twenty of the twenty-two **régions**.

Political debate and conflict fueled by ideological passions and exploding into street demonstrations are frequent in French public life. Politics is also a common topic of conversation when friends and family gather.

40. *GRANDEUR*

Grandeur was the heart of the concept of France that General Charles de Gaulle (1890–1970) developed to restore the self-confidence and pride of a country that had surrendered to the German army and had to accept Nazi occupation from 1940 to 1944. The Vichy regime (officially **l'État Français**) under Marshal Philippe Pétain (1856–1951) collaborated with Hitler during that time and carried out Hitler's policies in France, while General de Gaulle commanded the Free French Forces and the French Resistance from exile. Although de Gaulle's army played a relatively small role in the Allied liberation of Europe and Pétain's collaboration weakened France's moral position in the armistice, de Gaulle insisted that France be on an equal footing with the Soviet Union, the United Kingdom, and the United States at the Yalta Conference at the end of World War II.

De Gaulle was determined to have France play a leading role in world affairs independent of the two superpowers that emerged from Yalta, the United States and the Soviet Union. He identified **grandeur** with France's foreign policy as an independent nation of the world. His repeated affirmation of France's **grandeur** and democratic principles and his frequent opposition to "Anglo-Saxon" (American and British) foreign policy gave the French at home pride in their country's stature and achievements. The "Anglo-Saxons" were often irritated by his claims and behavior, which they regarded as unjustified and arrogant. The foreign image of French arrogance has resurfaced every time successive French presidents have taken a different view of world affairs to that of the American president. This happened once more in 2003 when President Jacques Chirac opposed the American-led invasion of Iraq and proposed multilateralism as a world policy instead of America's superpower unilateralism.

The need for **grandeur** in public life has become a French tradition along with a chauvinistic view of France as the center of the world.

41. GREETINGS AND FAREWELLS

The formal etiquette of shaking hands or kissing family members on both cheeks (**la bise**) when meeting or saying good-bye remains a core tradition that all French people observe. Even friends who use the informal **Salut!** as the accompanying greeting or farewell will shake hands or offer **la bise**.

When people are meeting for the first time or when they are of unequal social or professional status, the handshake is always used and the verbal greeting takes the form of **Bonjour, Madame/Monsieur/Mademoiselle**, without the person's name. The formal farewell is **Au revoir, Madame/Monsieur/Mademoiselle**. To greet a small group of people casually, the newcomer will often say **Bonjour (Salut), tout le monde!** (Hi, everyone!) Even in this casual situation, the newcomer will shake hands with those present. On leaving the group, **Au revoir (Salut), tout le monde!** (Good-bye, everyone!) is said.

The initial greeting is followed by a **de rigueur** question about the person's morale or health. Informally, the question is usually **Ça va?** Otherwise, a choice must be made between the formal **vous** and the friendly **tu: Vous allez bien?** or **Tu vas bien?** Foreigners in doubt should use the **vous** form and pay attention to whether their French acquaintance indicates the relationship has become informal or close enough to be at the **tu** stage—except in the case of student with student, which is invariably **tu** unless a speaker wants to signal a special reason for distance.

The greeting and farewell expressions in professional and personal letters are strictly codified in their levels of formality, which takes some getting used to. The most formal level, again, omits first and family names and begins with a bare **Monsieur, Madame**, or **Mademoiselle**. The addition of **cher** (**chère**) colors the formality with a shade of warmth. The first name is used in letters between family members and close friends: **Mon cher Pierre, Ma chère Isabelle**.

Farewell expressions in French letters strike English speakers used to "Yours sincerely" as particularly wordy, complex, and flowery. The form of address that appeared in the opening greeting reappears in the farewell at the end. Some examples, from very formal to relatively informal, are:

- **Veuillez agréer, Monsieur, l'expression de mes sentiments les plus distingués.** (Please be willing to accept, Sir, the expression of my most distinguished sentiments.)
- **Je vous prie de recevoir, cher Monsieur, l'expression de mes salutations les meilleures.** (I beg you to accept, dear Sir, the expression of my best greetings.)
- **Je t'envoie, ma chère Isabelle, mon amical souvenir.** (I send you, my dear Isabelle, my friendly remembrance.)
- **Je t'embrasse** or **Bises.** (Kisses.)

The first example is appropriate for most business letters to customers or suppliers or when applying for information, the second to colleagues or acquaintances, the third for friends, and the fourth for close friendships. When in doubt between two choices, foreigners should opt for the more formal of the two and observe the form that is used in the reply.

New Year wishes can be sent until 31 January and are expressed with similar levels of formality. Standard expressions are:

- **Je vous présente tous mes meilleurs vœux pour la Nouvelle Année.** (I present you with all my best wishes for the New Year.)
- **Je vous souhaite une très bonne et heureuse Nouvelle Année.** (I wish you a very good and happy New Year.)

42. GUILLOTINE

A professor of anatomy, Joseph Guillotin (1733–1814), invented a machine and proposed in 1789 that it be used to cut off the heads of the people that Revolutionary organizations condemned to death. The most famous victims of the guillotine were King Louis XVI (1754–93) and Queen Marie-Antoinette (1755–93), who were beheaded in public in 1793 on the square now called **Place de la Concorde** in Paris.

France continued to use the guillotine to execute criminals whom the courts condemned to death until the government of Socialist president François Mitterrand (1916–1996) abolished capital punishment in 1981.

43. HEALTH AND FITNESS

The French set great store by their health (**santé**), a fact that is not surprising in a nation that produced Louis Pasteur (1822–95), the prime discoverer of microbiology; the international humanitarian group of doctors **Médecins Sans Frontières** or **MSF** (Doctors Without Borders); and the research team at the **Institut Pasteur** under Luc Montagnier (1932–), who were the first to discover the AIDS virus. France spends 9 percent of the national budget on health, more than any of its European partners. In a 2005 survey asking what the French government's priorities should be in the national budget, health was number one, followed by employment and education.

The French visit their doctors frequently and expect a high level of service when they do, involving numerous prescriptions and medical examinations. The French are Europe's leading hypochondriacs, taking three times more prescription medicines, especially tranquilizers, sleeping pills, and antidepressants, than the Germans and British. The French national health system, part of the social security system (**la sécurité sociale**, often called **la "Sécu"**), was one of the earliest (1945) in Europe and reimburses 70 percent of every citizen's medical and hospital expenses. This generous social security system is very costly for the state. To reduce the system's huge financial deficit, which is partly caused by excessive visits to doctors, from 2005 on, patients have to chose one main doctor (**médecin traitant**) and pay one euro for each consultation. In addition, by 2007, to further restrict unnecessary visits to different doctors, every French person will have a computerized medical dossier detailing all consultations, treatments, and hospitalizations prescribed by the doctor and only these will be reimbursed.

For all the attention that the French demand of their doctors, they often prefer homeopathic treatments purchased from the pharmacist, herbal teas for stress or insomnia, and home remedies for various ailments. Many also believe in the beneficial effects of taking the cure at a spa such as Vichy or Évian. Mineral water from a spa is popular as a remedy for minor ills.

The French tend to speak in general terms about their health. Foreigners learn that **"Je suis fatigué(e)"** means "I am tired," but for French people this is often also a way of saying "I am not feeling well." The French do, however, have a preoccupation with the state of their livers. They announce proudly that they have had a liver attack (**avoir mal au foie**) probably because it is the result of enjoying too much good food and wine. It is generally recognized, however, that the usual French diet of well-balanced meals eaten at home and few sweets is very healthy. France has the lowest rate of cardiovascular disease in the European Union. Despite an antismoking campaign introduced by the government in 1992 and high taxes on cigarettes, smoking remains common in France but far less so than in Greece, Ireland, and Spain.

Keeping fit (**garder la forme**) has become a pastime for sedentary French city dwellers since the international fashion of aerobics and jogging began in the 1980s. When the French say **faire de la gym** or **faire du sport**, they often simply mean doing some aerobic exercises in a fitness center (**un gymnase** or **un club de sport**). The French have always enjoyed such healthy outdoor activities as country walking (**la randonnée**) and cycling (**faire du vélo**).

44. HEROES AND HEROINES

The French refer to their past much more and plan their future much less than Americans. Certain men and women have become legendary in French history for their exploits, and they often serve as examples, symbols, and proverbs in discussions and in news presentations.

Two examples of patriotism are Vercingétorix and Joan of Arc. Vercingétorix (72–46 B.C.) led the Gauls against the invading army of Julius Caesar, was defeated at Alésia in 52 B.C., and surrendered valiantly. Joan of Arc (**Jeanne d'Arc**, 1412–31) was inspired by saints' voices to lead a mission to drive the English out of France, rally the dispirited French forces, and in turn inspire the passive Charles VII (1403–61) to assert his kingship and triumph over the English, ending the Hundred Years' War.

King Louis XIV (1638–1715), the Sun King (**le Roi Soleil**), and Napoleon Bonaparte (1769–1821) are emblematic of French **grandeur** for expanding the role of France in Europe through a series of triumphs over competing nations. (The defeat of Napoleon by the English did not mitigate his lasting accomplishments as much as George IV and Wellington might have wished.) They bequeathed to French heritage, respectively, the Palace of Versailles and the Napoleonic legal code.

The French hero of the American Revolution, the Marquis de La Fayette (1757–1834), who sent President George Washington the key to the captured French Bastille from "a missionary of Liberty to its Patriarch," played a significant role in the French Revolution but is better known in the United States than in France.

The engineer Gustave Eiffel (1832–1923) designed the tower that bears his name for the World Exhibition of 1889. The Eiffel Tower (**la Tour Eiffel**) has come to be a symbol of Paris and sparkled with twenty thousand tiny white lights to announce the beginning of the twenty-first century.

Cyrano de Bergerac, the main character in the famous play (1897) of the same name by Edmond Rostand (1868–1918), represents the French ideal of overcoming adversity with daring and panache, not to mention wit.

The Polish-born Marie Sklodowska Curie (1867–1934), together with her physicist husband Pierre (1859–1906), discovered radium. She won the Nobel Prize jointly with him and Henri Becquerel in 1903 and alone in 1911. She was the first woman member of the **Académie de Médecine**.

Charles de Gaulle (1890–1970) fled to London after the German invasion in 1940 and organized the Free French Movement, which supported the **Résistance** against the Nazis in France. He led the liberation of Paris in 1944.

Many French heroes, including literary giants such as Voltaire, Jean-Jacques Rousseau, Victor Hugo, Émile Zola, and André Malraux, have been given the highest honor of burial in the **Panthéon**, an imposing domed mausoleum in Paris's Latin Quarter (**Quartier Latin**). The crowds of tourists visiting it will notice that only two women are buried there: Marie Curie (in 1995) and Sophie Berthelot (in 1907, because she died only hours after her husband Marcellin Berthelot, a chemist).

A popular hero who is a symbol of French defiance, but who will not be buried in the **Panthéon**, is Astérix, the **bande dessinée** (comic-book) character created by René Goscinny and Albert Uderzo and modeled on France's first patriot, Vercingétorix. (By the way, the French are avid readers of **bandes dessinées**).

The visitor to France may occasionally hear reference to **Marianne**, the name the French have bestowed on the female emblem of liberty and the symbol of the Republic. Actors Brigitte Bardot, Catherine Deneuve, and Sophie Marceau, the model Laetitia Casta, and the television talk-show host Evelyne Thomas have served as models for the plaster sculpture of **Marianne**, wearing a Revolutionary bonnet, that is found inside every city hall in France and on stamps.

45. HEXAGON

The French often refer to their country as the Hexagon (**l'Hexagone**) because France has roughly a six-sided shape. Hexagonal behavior or

FRANCE: A HEXAGON OF TWENTY-TWO REGIONS

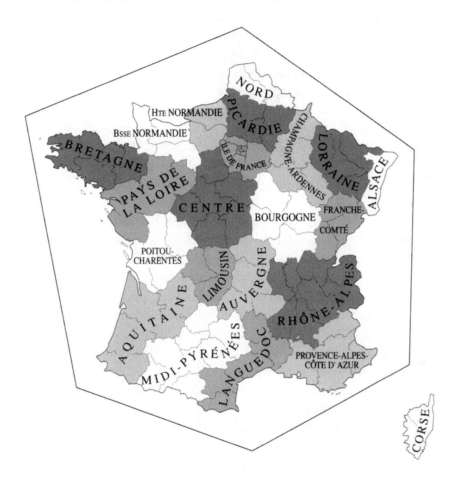

attitudes are those that look inward nationalistically and exclude foreign points of view and influences.

46. HIGH TECH

Daily life in France today is being rapidly transformed by high technology (**le high-tech**) and the digital revolution (**la révolution numérique**). It took thirty years for all French homes to have a television set and fifteen years for half of French homes to have a computer. The first DVD players (**lecteurs de DVD**) appeared in France in 1999. Six years later, 80 percent of all homes had one. The must-have presents for Christmas 2004 were a digital music player (**un baladeur numérique**) or a flat-screen television (**une télévision à écran plat**). In 2005, 75 percent of the population had a mobile phone (**un [téléphone] portable**), and, in the first three months of that year, they sent over three million text messages (**textos**).

The French have always been fascinated by technical inventions. The **Minitel**, a French-invented computer system linked through telephone lines, was introduced in 1983. It was limited to France but the popularity of its directory services both at home and for business made the French slow to adopt the Internet. At the beginning of 2004, a quarter of French homes were connected to the Web (**la toile**) compared with 36 percent in Great Britain and 47 percent in Germany. In 1974, a Parisian, Roland Moreno (1945–) invented a "smartcard" that contains a microchip (**une puce**) to debit charges from the customer's bank or credit account at the point of purchase. Gemplus, a French company near Marseille (in southern France), is the world leader in smartcards. In 2002, a smartcard called **Monéo** was introduced for small purchases like a cup of coffee.

Computerized home appliances and vending machines, commercial laser lighting effects, and advanced telecommunication equipment are now commonplace in France. In the transportation area, the **TGV** (**train à grande vitesse**; high-speed train), the **VAL** (**véhicule automatique léger**; driverless metro train), the driverless minibus (part of a European project called **Cybercar-Cybermove**, to encourage use of public transportation in cities), and the Airbus airplanes use the latest technology.

In space technology, France has a majority share in the European Space Agency, which launches communication satellites from the space center at Kourou in French Guiana (**la Guyane**). The first Ariane rocket was launched from there in 1979, which established Europe's technological independence in the space industry. In 2005, Arianespace successfully launched the new version of the Ariane 5 rocket, capable of lifting a ten-ton satellite into space. In 2005, the European Space Agency also launched the navigation system satellite **Galileo** to break the monopoly of the U.S. miltary–controlled satellite GPS. Cadarache (in southern France) was chosen in 2005 as the construction site for ITER, the international project to develop tomorrow's electricity-producing fusion power plants.

47. HOLIDAYS

All countries have traditional holidays, usually inspired by a mixture of history, religion, and paganism, and France is no exception. What is noticeable in France's case is the richness and variety of its **fêtes** (festivals): the way they point to its Catholic heritage, the French love of food and their rural past, and the Revolutionary tradition.

Traditional observances that are not linked to public holidays (**jours fériés**) are:

• Epiphany—**L'Epiphanie** (6 January). The French celebrate the Three Kings by buying a special cake, **la galette des rois**, sold for several weeks around the holiday at bakeries and supermarkets. The **galette** comes with a gold paper crown and conceals a tiny ceramic figure, **la fève** (bean, which it originally was). The cake is solemnly cut for dessert, and the person whose slice contains **la fève** is crowned king or queen and chooses a royal partner.

• Carnival—**Le Carnaval** (Between Epiphany and Mardi Gras, the last day before Lent, usually in late February). Many regions hold carnivals, which feature costumed processions and masked parades. The city of Nice holds the biggest carnival.

• **La Chandeleur** (2 February). On this feast of the Virgin, it is traditional to eat pancakes (**crêpes**) at home.

• Valentine's Day—**La Saint-Valentin** (14 February). Valentine's Day was not especially celebrated by the French. In 1990, the newspaper *Libération* began publishing Valentine's Day messages. This has now become a popular custom as well as lovers sending St. Valentine text messages over their mobile phones.

• Saint Patrick's Day—**La fête de Saint-Patrick** (17 March). This Irish holiday, with its beer-drinking tradition, is the most popular foreign national day in France. Its popularity is associated with the revival of Celtic culture, particularly in Brittany where each summer the Interceltic Festival in the city of Lorient attracts well over half a million people.

• April Fools—**Le premier avril** (1 April). This is a day for mischievous pranks. Children cut out paper fish (**poissons d'avril**) and attach them to people's backs.

• Mother's Day, Father's Day—**La fête des mères** is celebrated on a Sunday in May and **la fête des pères** on a Sunday in June. The occasion is celebrated with gifts and family get-togethers. Mother's Day is the more widely observed.

• Music Day—**La fête de la Musique** (21 June). Dating from 1982, this popular celebration of music with open-air concerts and informal street performances by musicians coincides with the starting date of summer on the calendar.

• Halloween—**Halloween** (31 October). The French began celebrating Halloween in 1997 as part of a publicity campaign using pumpkins (**citrouilles**). Since then, Halloween disguises have become popular with children and some stores decorate their windows with Halloween symbols.

Les jours fériés, official national holidays, have a civil or religious inspiration:

- New Year's Day—**Le Jour de l'An** (1 January). New Year's Eve, **la Saint-Sylvestre**, is the occasion for parties and late-night feasting (**le réveillon**) with friends and family. At midnight, celebrating drivers herald the new year with a cacophony of car horns.

- Easter Monday—**Le lundi de Pâques**. At Easter, shops sell items that commemorate the holiday's Christian origins as well as pagan symbols of fertility—eggs, bells, fish, and rabbits made of chocolate.

- Labor Day—**La fête du Travail** (1 May). Since 1947, trade unions organize marches and many people buy sprigs of lily-of-the-valley (**le muguet**) to give to family and friends with a wish for happiness.

- V.E. Day—**La fête de la Victoire** (8 May). Victory in Europe Day celebrates the end of World War II in 1945. In 2005, huge celebrations across Europe marked the sixtieth anniversary of the defeat of Hitler and German Nazism and the end of the Holocaust.

- Ascension Thursday—**L'Ascension** (Forty days after Easter, usually in May). Few people now go to church on this religious holiday.

- Whitsun Monday—**Le lundi de Pentecôte** (Fifty days after Easter). The Monday following Whit Sunday was a public holiday until 2005, when, after an abnormally high number of old people died during a severe heatwave in August 2003, the government decided that it would be a working day called **La journée de la solidarité**. A percentage of workers' pay on that day is allocated to a national solidarity fund for aged and disabled citizens. Despite the government decision, a large number of workers continued the tradition of the day as a public holiday.

- National Day ("Bastille Day")—**La fête nationale, le Quatorze Juillet** (14 July). This anniversary of the storming of the Bastille in 1789 strikes a chord in every French heart and is the occasion of military processions, fireworks, and open-air balls. This patriotic day celebrating the French Republic also marks the beginning of the summer vacation period.

• Assumption—**L'Assomption** (15 August). The taking of Mary into heaven has been forgotten by many French people as they treat this holiday as a bonus attached to the beginning or end of their summer vacation. On this day, the **autoroutes** are doubly crowded with vacationers leaving for or returning from vacation spots.

• All Saints' Day—**La Toussaint** (1 November). The French commemorate their dead, particularly family members, on this day by going to the cemetery and placing chrysanthemums on the family graves. Church leaders have criticized the growing popularity of Halloween, which has caused a decline in the religious observance of **Toussaint** the following day.

• Armistice Day—**L'Armistice** (11 November). This day marks the date of the armistice that brought an end to World War I in 1918.

• Christmas—**Noël** (25 December). This holiday is very much a family holiday. On Christmas Eve, religiously inclined people attend midnight Mass and the whole family stays up late for **le réveillon**, a lavish traditional meal for which no expense is spared. Traditional foods are **le pâté de foie gras**, oysters, smoked salmon, turkey, and **la bûche de Noël** (a chocolate-coated cake in the form of a log), with champagne. Churches display Nativity crib scenes, and in the south live lambs are placed near the cribs during midnight Mass. Children leave out shoes rather than stockings to receive gifts from **le Père Noël** (Father Christmas).

The Jewish festival of Yom Kippur and the feast of Aïd, which is celebrated at the end of Ramadan by the large Muslim community in France, are respected but are not public holidays.

Often weekends in May are long weekends because a public holiday falls on a Friday or a Monday. When it falls on a Thursday (which is always the date of Ascension) or a Tuesday, many French people make the bridge (**faire le pont**) to the weekend and take an extra day off work.

48. HOUSING

Most inhabitants of French cities live in apartment buildings, but 56 percent of the population lives in houses. Fifty-five percent of families own their homes, and almost a quarter of the family budget is spent on the home to pay for rent (where applicable), furnishings, household goods, and decorating. Since the 1980s, homes have become more spacious and more comfortable. The introduction of the thirty-five hour workweek in 1998 and new technologies making it possible to work from home have meant that people are spending more time in their homes, and they are reorganizing its layout and decorating it for more comfortable living. The privacy of one's home (**chez soi**) has always been very important to the French, who prefer to invite only close friends to their homes. They meet with other friends and acquaintances in **cafés** and restaurants.

The **concierge**, guardian of the entrance to the apartment building and traditional institution of French life, is disappearing. Modern buildings have replaced **la concierge** with **le gardien** or **la gardienne**. The mail carrier (**le facteur**) now puts the mail in personal letter boxes at the entrance to the building and visitors gain entrance through an intercom. To increase security against housebreakings and robberies, many buildings have installed a number-code lock (**digicode**) on the street entrance door. This code (**code**) is changed from time to time, and residents and visitors must know it in order to enter the building after 8:00 P.M.

The population explosion led by the post–World War II baby boomers, together with a large population movement from rural life to city life, and the immigration of foreign workers has caused a rapid expansion of the suburbs around the cities. The state has had to construct cheap high-rise housing apartments (**habitations à loyer modéré**, or **HLM**).

Today more than three million families live in these unattractive, often dilapidated public-housing tower blocks built on the periphery of cities and towns. These high-density apartment blocks are grouped together forming **cités** (housing projects) where the majority of inhabitants are Muslim, working-class families with a large number of children who, if they are born in France, have French nationality. Some **cités** are now like segregated, deprived ghettos with prevalent crime. High rates of youth unemployment (up to 40 percent for young people aged eighteen to twenty-five, whereas the national average for this age group is 22.9 percent), poverty, and exclusion are among the reasons for antisocial behavior, outbreaks of violence, and clashes with the police. The long-standing French immigration policy of assimilation declares that, once in France, legal immigrants are French and everyone is equal.

Clashes between young people and the police in the **cités** in the suburbs of Paris and of the major provincial cities were intermittent. They turned into three weeks of nightly riots led by angry young **beurs** in October and November 2005 after two teenage **beurs** were accidentally electrocuted while fleeing a police security check in the northern Paris suburb of Clichy-sous-Bois. Nicolas Sarkozy, the minister for police and security, commented that the rioters were scum (**racaille**), inflaming the riots which spread to the suburbs with large immigrant populations throughout France. The majority of rioting **beurs** were teenagers and French citizens who were protesting inequities and pervasive discrimination in French society, notably regarding employment. They frequently cited discrimination as the reason for not being hired because of their Arab or African names and their home addresses. Riot police were pelted, more than one hundred public buildings such as schools and community sports centers were set on fire, shops were attacked, and buses and more than nine thousand cars were torched, but there was only one death (a pensioner who was punched by a rioter). It was the worst urban civil unrest in France since the events of May 1968.

To stop the riots, the government reinforced its policy of law and order by declaring a state of emergency that lasted from 8 November to 4 January. It allowed police searches without warrants and an evening curfew to be imposed on juveniles in some **cités**. Rioters who did not have French nationality were deported. Measures were introduced to promote social cohesion and to improve employment opportunities for young people living in **cités** by creating a civilian service agency to provide employment and training to fifty thousand young people by 2007. The European Union offered France fifty million euros to help recover from the damage to property done during the rioting.

France holds the current world record for the percentage of families who own a holiday home (**une résidence secondaire**)—10 percent. Most of these families belong to the upper class, live in the city, and use the home for weekends and vacations. The demand has been met by a great many country houses that have gone up for sale as much of France's previously large rural population has migrated to the city.

The economic recession in the 1980s and its resulting unemployment created a phenomenon to which France had been unaccustomed: the homeless (**SDF**, short for **les sans domicile fixe**; or **les sans-abri**). Paris has always had a few **clochards** (tramps) who slept under the city's bridges and were a picturesque and not unsettling part of the tourist's view of the romantic Seine. It is estimated that there are now ninety thousand homeless people, and begging on the streets is common. It is also estimated that 3.5 million people, including one million children, live in poverty. A priest, the abbé Pierre (1912–), has become a popular folk hero through his work with the poor and homeless, which has included residences (**auberges Emmaüs**) for them. He and the popular comedian Coluche (1944–86) joined forces in 1985 to set up **les restos** (restaurants) **du cœur**, soup kitchens that provide free meals and help to the poor and homeless during winter. When **les restos du cœur** celebrated their twentieth anniversary in 2005, they were serving sixty-six million meals annually. The French give willingly to charitable causes, and in 2004, five million French households gave on average 250 euros each to charities.

49. HUMOR

French humor is often described as being more intellectual and analytical than either English humor, which ranges from understatement and self-deprecation to silly fun, or American humor, which favors deadpan absurdity, poking fun at public figures, and veiled allusions to items of popular culture. The French have an instinctive fear of appearing ridiculous but enjoy slapstick movies.

The French word **esprit** means both "the mind" and "wit" (humor). The French enjoy telling witty anecdotes that play with words rather than dirty jokes, and comedians performing satirical sketches are popular. An example of humorous playing with the sound of words is the series of cat drawings using the sound of the word **chat** (cat) to form many other words that contain that syllable, such as **chapeau** (hat). A similar play on sounds plays with hearers' misinterpretations, as in the tongue-twister (really more accurately an ear-twister), **Si six scies scient six cyprès, six cents scies scient six cents cyprès** (If six saws saw six cypresses, six hundred saws saw six hundred cypresses). This sounds like complete gibberish (**si-si-si-si-si cyprès** . . .) until the hearer identifies the word **scie**.

Another popular French comic tradition is exaggerated caricature and farce, like the mock-epic adventures of Gargantua and Pantagruel written by Rabelais (c. 1494–1553). Many popular French movies, such as one of the biggest French box-office hits, **Les Visiteurs** (1992), are outlandish farces that continue the Rabelaisian tradition and satirize the pretentiousness and ridiculous conventions of contemporary society.

The French enjoy comic books (**bandes dessinées**, or **BD** for short) so much that they have elevated them to an art form. All young children know the numerous adventures of Tintin and his dog Milou, a comic strip that began in 1929. They and their parents are also avid readers of the Astérix books, which started in 1959. Astérix, France's best-loved comic book character, is a Gaul, like the hero Vercingétorix who led the resistance to the Roman invasion of Gaul (France). The characters besides Astérix (whose name plays on the word **astérisque**) are his side-kick Obélix (playing on **obélisque**, "obelisk"), the village poet Assurancetourix (playing on **assurance tous risques**, "comprehensive insurance"), and the tribal chief Abraracourix (playing on **à bras raccourcis**, "with all one's force"). The adventures use settings from Roman times, but readers recognize the comic transposition of current events and attitudes in the setting, and the forays of Astérix into Roman Britain, Germany, Italy, and so on provide opportunities for readers to enjoy seeing fun poked at France's contemporary neighbors. Astérix represents the patriotic Frenchman who uses intelligence and native cunning to withstand the threats to his survival and pride from ambitious foreign countries and their ideas. The thirty-second annual International Comic Book Festival (**Festival international de la BD**) was held in the city of Angoulême (in the center of France) in 2005.

Politics has a special fascination for the French, and much of their humor is politically inspired. A popular television program is *Les Guignols de l'info*, in which puppets caricature leading political personalities. Political satire has made a long-standing success of the weekly newspaper *Le Canard enchaîné*.

50. IMMIGRATION

Since the French Revolution, all governments except the Vichy government during World War II have maintained the tradition of France as a country offering political asylum to all people forced to flee for safety from their homelands. This has earned France a reputation as **"le pays des Droits de l'Homme"** ("the land of human rights"). In 2004, France had the highest number of applications from asylum seekers in the world. During this century, France has provided homes to White Russians (anti-Bolsheviks); anti-Fascist Italians; Republican Spaniards; Jews fleeing Nazism; Hungarians, Czechs, and Slovaks fleeing reprisals after their failed attempts to oust Stalinist Communism; and Southeast Asians fleeing the dangers of Vietnam and Cambodia.

Workers from Poland and Italy entered France between World Wars I and II to work in French mines and heavy industries. Other immigrant workers, since World War II, provided cheap labor for the thirty years of France's powerful economic growth called **les trente glorieuses** (the thirty glorious years) from 1946 to 1975. Africans and Arabs from France's former colonies have joined Portuguese and Spaniards in forming the mass of unskilled workers in agriculture and industry. The French automobile industry in particular has depended on this workforce for its expansion. Some of the immigrant workers, especially those from continental Europe, are seasonal agricultural laborers.

In the 2004 census, 9.6 percent of the population in mainland France were immigrants aged eighteen and over, and a third of them lived in the Paris region. It was estimated that there could be as many as one million illegal immigrants, called **clandestins** or **sans-papiers**. France is one of the thirteen European Union countries between which there are no border controls and that constitute the Schengen Zone. Great Britain and Ireland are not part of the Schengen Zone. Stricter controls for entry into the Schengen Zone have decreased the number of illegal immigrants.

Africans outnumber Europeans in the immigrant population. Almost six hundred thousand immigrants come from both Algeria and Portugal; over five hundred thousand from Morocco; just under four hundred thousand from Italy; just over three hundred thousand from Spain; two hundred thousand from Tunisia; and less than two hundred thousand from Turkey. The majority of immigrants are from the three North African countries called **le Maghreb: l'Algérie, le Maroc**, and **la Tunisie**. They are mostly Muslim.

The large number of these immigrants, their different religions and customs, and rising unemployment have made them an object of racist attacks, especially by the extreme right-wing National Front party. The children of the immigrants from **le Maghreb** who are born and live in France are called **beurs**. They have French nationality if they are born in France and, like all French children, are integrated into the French educational system with its republican secular values in public schools. It was on these principles that the wearing of conspicuous signs of religion, in particular the wearing of headscarves by Muslim girls, was banned by law in 2004.

France's immigration policy has been based on integration by assimilation, called **le modèle républicain** (the republican model). Assimilation is the unifying ideal of the French Republic. The victory of the French team in the World Soccer Cup in 1998 helped change attitudes about immigrants. Some members of the team had black African origins, and the champion goal scorer, Zinédine Zidane, whose family had migrated from Morocco, became a national hero. A new image of France as **"black, blanc, beur"** emerged, but incidents of racist, anti–Arab-immigrant and anti-Semitic behavior continued to occur, influenced by the far right policies of the National Front. The three weeks of suburban rioting in October and November 2005 (see Housing) revealed that the French Republic's policy of integration by assimilation was failing.

51. *JE T'AIME, JE T'ADORE*

Je t'aime (I love you) and **je t'adore** (I adore you) are frequently spoken by lovers to express their affection for each other. France and Paris have a worldwide reputation for love and romance. French people do not hide their emotions from the public gaze. Amorous encounters take place in open-air **cafés**, and park benches attract necking couples. The women's movement in France did not change French women's expectations to be courted and paid compliments. A popular saying in France is that **l'amour** (love) rhymes with **toujours** (always). France has given English the expression **amour fou** (madly in love).

Having a romance with a French person is an exotic fantasy for many foreigners, whose imagination is titillated by stereotypes that the French spend their time making love, that French men are the best lovers, and that French women are the sexiest.

French history and art have helped build the exaggerated image. The twelfth-century theologian Abélard and his lover Héloïse, who became a nun, lived out the quintessential story of the star-crossed lovers. The leading existentialists Jean-Paul Sartre (1905–80) and Simone de Beauvoir (1908–86) carried on a lifelong open relationship before the eyes of the world. The accordion strains of many Parisian love songs have graced romantic Hollywood movies and elegant restaurants with subdued lighting. A large proportion of the French films exported to other countries have a love plot. The Folies Bergère and the cabarets in Pigalle as well as the Lido on the Champs-Élysées and its neighbor, the Crazy Horse Saloon, have also made their contributions to tourists' impressions of erotic Paris.

52. *JOIE DE VIVRE*

Joie de vivre (joy of living) is a French expression adopted into English. The French enjoy having fun and making the most of happy occasions. They are hardworking and serious at their professions, but, during their leisure time, they are keen to relax. Making time for leisurely meals and gathering with family and friends in a convivial atmosphere where work is forgotten, with plenty of jokes and laughter, is very much part of the French lifestyle.

The famous high-kicking dance, **le can-can**, expresses the feisty abandonment of decorum in pursuit of good-tempered fun that has become an international image of French **joie de vivre**.

53. KILOS

The metric system of weights and measures was invented in France. Before the Revolution, the units of measure varied from province to province. In 1790, the Constituent Assembly instructed the Academy of Sciences to establish a unit of measure that would be valid for all peoples at all times. The metric system was introduced in 1795 and became legal in 1799.

Solids are measured in **grammes** and **kilogrammes**, or **kilos**. The **gramme** is used for items sold in small quantities, such as spices. Expensive items, such as meats and chocolates, have prices quoted by **cent grammes** (100 **grammes**). Items such as butter, fruit, and vegetables are sold and priced by the **demi-kilo** (500 **grammes**; half-kilo), which is called **une livre** (a pound).

Body weight is measured in **kilos** and **grammes**. Especially with the current fashion of exercising and diet to keep fit and slim, **kilos** is often heard in the expressions **prendre des kilos** and **perdre des kilos** (which mean "to put on [excessive] weight" and "to lose [excessive] weight," respectively).

54. KISSING

Foreigners comment that the French spend a lot of time kissing each other on the cheeks. Family members and close friends, both male and female, kiss each other on both cheeks (the gesture is called **la bise**) when they meet and when they part company. The form of **la bise** varies from region to region and with closer intimacy: from one kiss on each cheek starting with the right cheek, to one kiss on each cheek and a third on the first cheek, to twice on both cheeks.

On formal occasions, men of the upper bourgeoisie and aristocracy may kiss the hand of a married woman instead of shaking her hand to greet and say farewell. This custom is disappearing along with other rules of rigid etiquette.

Kissing on the lips is erotic and is only for lovers.

Some language notes are in order. The verb for "to kiss" is **embrasser**, or **s'embrasser** (to kiss each other). The noun is **un baiser**. There is a verb **baiser** that often confuses foreigners because the French never use it to mean "to kiss"; rather, it means "to screw."

55. LEISURE

Since 2001, the French workweek has been thirty-five hours and the legal retirement age sixty or, for some categories of workers, fifty-five. French leisure time has increased as a result, but, for many retirees, this has meant more time watching television. In 2003, the French spent on average three hours and twenty-two minutes each day watching television, with women spending more time (three hours and forty-three minutes) than men (three hours and nineteen minutes). It is estimated that the adult population spends six and half hours a day on media leisure activities (which are sometimes done simultaneously). In addition to watching television, they spend one hour and fifty-seven minutes listening to the radio and thirty-seven minutes reading newspapers and magazines as well as searching the Internet.

Leisure activities can be divided between cultural pursuits (such as watching television; reading; listening to music; going to the movies, theater, and concerts; visiting museums and art exhibitions; and engaging in photography) and simple relaxation activities (such as playing sports, walking, fishing, hunting, playing cards, and dancing in clubs). The French rarely concentrate on only one of these two types of leisure activities. They mix both in accordance with the precept of the sixteenth-century philosopher Michel de Montaigne (1533–92) that an active mind needs to be balanced by a healthy body. In 2001, just over 50 percent of the family budget for cultural activities was spent on leisure time involving sound and image (television, radio, CDs, DVDs, movies, photography). Twenty-four percent was spent on reading activities, and 23 percent on buying tickets for shows and theme parks (Disneyland Paris, the Futuroscope at Poitiers, Astérix Park north of Paris), going to discos, and visiting museums and monuments. In 2004, one in four French people played video games and spent on average two hours and forty-five minutes playing them each week. In 2005, 60 percent of the population owned a DVD player. In 2003, 54 percent bought at least one book, and reading (including newspapers and magazines) was the second most frequent pastime after watching television. Today, a large number of cultural purchases are made in **hypermarchés** (huge supermarkets). In 2003, 18.9 percent of books, 42.3 percent of CDs, and 70 percent of DVDs and videos were bought there.

Walking in the countryside and bike riding (**faire du vélo**) have long been popular pastimes for all ages. More recently, inline skating (**faire du roller**) has become popular for younger people. Some relaxation activities are home related. French men report that 80 percent of them do household repairs, and 60 percent of all French people do some form of gardening. The French are keen collectors, and 23 percent of the population over the age of fifteen have some kind of collection, the largest group (8 percent) being stamp collectors.

There is a photo camera (**un appareil [photographique]**) in 90 percent of French homes and a video camera (**un caméscope**) in more than 20 percent. The earliest photographic processes were French. Nicéphore Niepce (1765–1833) developed a process in 1826, and Louis Jacques Daguerre (1787–1851), for whom the daguerreotype was named, refined it and sold the patent to the state in 1839. Among the most influential twentieth-century photographers was Henri Cartier-Bresson (1908–2004), who cofounded the famous Magnum Photo Agency. The Jeu de Paume Museum in the Paris Tuileries Gardens is the national museum of photography.

56. *LIBERTÉ, ÉGALITÉ, FRATERNITÉ*

"Liberty, equality, fraternity" was the rallying cry of the French Revolutionaries when they stormed the Bastille prison in 1789 and brought an end to the oppression, inequalities, and privileges of the absolute monarchy. The slogan originated when the *Journal de Paris* appealed to the public to print these words on their homes. Since the founding of the First Republic in 1792, **"Liberté, Égalité, Fraternité"** has been the motto of the French Republic and is displayed on public buildings. Respect for individual liberties has been one of the great republican ideals. **Egalité** is increasingly being interpreted in today's fractured society to mean **egalité des chances** (equality of opportunity). **Fraternité** has come to mean mutual support of all groups in the community; that is, it is roughly synonymous with solidarity.

Many national independence movements of the nineteenth and twentieth centuries adopted the slogan in their struggles to overthrow oppressive regimes.

The famous Statue of Liberty, standing at the entrance to New York since 1886, represents Liberty Enlightening the World. It was designed by a Frenchman, Frédéric-Auguste Bartholdi (1834–1904), and built in Paris from 1875 to 1884 before its journey across the Atlantic. Originally intended to mark one hundred years of Franco-American friendship since the Declaration of Independence, it has come to symbolize the values of freedom and democracy.

57. LOGIC

The French pride themselves in being logical in their thinking and rational in their behavior, characteristics that trace back to the French philosopher René Descartes (1596–1650), who postulated that intellect is humanity's distinguishing characteristic. Descartes's radical reduction of evidence in his philosophy to **"Je pense, donc je suis"** ("I think, therefore I am") began an analytical tradition known as Cartesian logic. Voltaire (1694–1778) and other eighteenth-century philosophers who inspired the Age of Enlightenment, in which all fields of social and political endeavor were subjected to critical inquiry, drew on Cartesian principles. This form of rationalism has continued as a dominant strain in French philosophy to the present time.

The Cartesian influence can be seen in many aspects of daily French life. A young child who misbehaves is told to be **raisonnable** (reasonable). Schools practice a rational approach to learning that stresses the ability to memorize, think clearly, and discuss abstract ideas. High intellectual performance is valued above sporting or civic achievements. The final high school examination, **le baccalauréat**, includes philosophy as one of the subjects and emphasizes rhetorical skills and deductive reasoning.

Intellectuals form a distinctive group in French society. They are admired for their abstract knowledge and their skill in challenging existing beliefs. They are also respected opinion makers, and news media often publish or broadcast interviews with them.

It has been said that the French prefer the exchange of ideas and a long discussion about the theoretical principles of a project to making a decision to act; that the educational system that favors intellectual over practical and vocational outcomes has restricted France's development in industry, commerce, and technology; and that more pragmatic peoples can achieve consensus more efficiently, because French discussions bring about ideological conflicts that delay decision making. The French would object that by daring to be different and by challenging solutions based on mere expediency, they are having a positive influence on the way the world thinks.

58. MARRIAGE AND DIVORCE

French couples often celebrate two separate marriage ceremonies because of the separation of church and state that has existed since 1905. The civil ceremony is obligatory and takes place at the city hall (**la mairie**). The marriage assumes legal status by this ceremony, which the mayor records in **le livret de famille** (family booklet) given to the newlyweds. The couple's children are recorded in the **livret** that serves as a legal document for the children until they reach adulthood at age eighteen. If the couple wants a religious wedding ceremony, it follows the civil ceremony.

The number of marriages per year has declined by over a third since 1975. This decline in a traditionally Catholic country reveals the weakening influence of the Church in France. Marriage is no longer seen by many French people as a religious and social institution but as a personal decision. In 2003, there were 280,300 marriages with the average age for men at the time of their marriage being thirty and four months and for women twenty eight and three months. In one-fifth of the marriages, one of the partners was not French. Over a quarter of French women have never married by the age of thirty-five.

Despite the fall in the marriage rate, the divorce rate has increased. Today almost half of French marriages end in divorce. The most frequent reason for divorce is unfaithfulness (**infidélité**). A public opinion survey in 2004 showed that 40 percent of men and 25 percent of women cheat on their partners, in the case of women three times higher than in the 1970s. A 2004 law made the procedure for divorce by mutual consent easier.

An estimated 15 percent of couples living together are unmarried. If they decide to get married, it is often to legitimize the children they have had and to qualify for tax advantages. More than four out of ten children have unmarried parents. Over 60 percent of couples who marry lived together as an unmarried couple before their marriage.

Marriage is declining, but the **PACS** (**le pacte civil de solidarité**), which became law at the end of 1999, is increasingly popular. A **PACS** is a civil contract registered at city hall establishing a legally binding partnership between couples of any sexual orientation. The 100,000th **PACS** was celebrated in December 2003. Opponents of the **PACS** law saw it as official recognition of homosexual relationships. In fact, a large number of **PACS** have been registered by heterosexual couples.

Same-sex marriage is illegal in France. France's first marriage of two gay men was celebrated by the mayor, a leading ecologist, in the southwestern town of Bègles in June 2004. After being declared illegal by the justice minister because France's civil code did not permit same-sex marriages, the courts declared it null and void because "the traditional function of marriage is commonly considered to be the founding of a family." Attitudes are, however, changing. In a 2004 survey for *Elle* magazine, 64 percent of respondents were in favor of same-sex couples having the right to marry. In a 1996 survey, only 48 percent were.

The number of single people has risen to such a degree that they now form a distinct social group. In 2003, there were fourteen million of them, an increase of five million since 2000.

59. *LA MARSEILLAISE*

The French national anthem was originally a war march composed in 1792 by Captain Claude Rouget de Lisle (1760–1836) while he was garrisoned in Strasbourg. The Marseille National Guard sang it as they entered Paris in July of that year, inspiring French patriotism with its stirring music, and thus it became known as **"La Marseillaise."** The opening two lines are:

Allons, enfants de la patrie
Le jour de gloire est arrivé.
Let's go, children of the homeland
The day of glory has arrived.

The battle call is repeated in each refrain:

Aux armes, citoyens! Formez vos bataillons!
Marchons! Marchons!
Take up your weapons, citizens! Form your battalions!
Let's march! Let's march!

Napoleon's (1791–1821) victorious armies made the French national anthem famous across Europe. Today, two centuries after its composition, it still symbolizes revolutionary fervor and patriotism for the French wherever they are in the world, especially on their national day, 14 July.

60. MEALS

Dinner (**le dîner**) has become the main French meal of the day. Lunch (**le déjeuner**), which used to be a traditional two-hour break, has generally been replaced in cities by a one-hour lunch. In some regional towns, the two-hour lunch break still exists. Sunday lunch remains a long meal at which family and friends often gather. Breakfast (**le petit déjeuner**) is a rapid meal often consisting of only bread, butter, and jam with a bowl of coffee or perhaps tea, or hot chocolate for young children. Only young children tend to have any snacks between meals, and even that is formalized as the after-school **goûter**.

Main meals traditionally have at least three courses, an introductory **hors d'œuvre**, a main course (**plat principal**), and cheese and/or dessert, accompanied by bread, wine, and mineral water. Young people are drinking less wine. The percentage of fruit juice drinkers rose from 25.6 percent in 1996 to 31.6 percent in 2002. For dinner, the **hors d'œuvre** is often soup. If the main course is meat, it is served with vegetables, rice, or pasta. A green salad may be served before the cheese, which is followed by fruit or dessert. A yogurt (**yaourt**) might replace cheese and dessert.

Simple main courses are steak and fries (**le biftek frites**) or chicken and fries (**le poulet frites**). Other favorites are blanquette of veal (**la blanquette de veau**) with rice, chicken in red wine (**le coq au vin**) with boiled potatoes, and beef stew (**le pot au feu**) with mixed vegetables.

The range of courses will strike an American or Briton as unusual. Visitors to France should prepare to be surprised with dishes such as **la bouillabaisse** (fish soup), **les endives** (Belgian endive), **les asperges** (asparagus), **le boudin blanc** (a delicately flavored white sausage similar to the German bockwurst), or **le lapin** (rabbit).

Today the French spend less time at the meal table during the workweek. Meals have become simpler, and there is a tendency to have only two courses. Less time is spent preparing meals. One reason is that 75 percent of the female population between the ages of twenty and sixty are working women.

A family rule is that children and parents eat the evening meal together and discuss the day's events at school and at work. More French people now leave the television on during meals. The evening French television news and weather report is at 8:00 P.M.

Table manners are generally more formal than in America, with wrists and arms resting on the edge of the table and not in the lap. Before beginning to eat the meal, people wish each other **Bon appétit** (Good appetite). Americans might be surprised during the meal to see the fork replace the knife in the right hand and a small piece of bread used by the left hand to push food onto the fork before it is carried to the mouth. When the main course is served, you do not begin eating until you are told to start while your meal is hot and not wait until everyone is served. Bread-and-butter plates are not used. The crusty French bread is placed on the table beside the plate you eat from. Bread is not eaten with butter or margarine; butter is plentiful in regions like Normandy but is eaten only with some varieties of cheese like Camembert and blue cheese.

The same plate, after being wiped clean with bread, can be used for the lettuce salad after the main course, but a new plate is usually used for cheese if it is not separated from the main course by a lettuce salad. Formal etiquette requires that a knife and fork be used to peel and eat fruit, such as apples and pears, for dessert.

61. MEDIA

The average television viewing time is about three hours and twenty-two minutes per day in France. In the United States, it is four hours and twenty-eight minutes.

Until 1982, television and radio were both a state monopoly in France. Since then, the public and private sectors have both been involved. A government-appointed body, the **Conseil supérieur de l'audiovisuel** (**CSA**) ensures that broadcasters respect the rules on which their licenses have been granted and protects their independence from political pressures. Free television can be watched on five of the six national networks. Three are state-financed channels: **France 2** and **France 3** provide news and a full range of programs, with **France 3** oriented to regional audiences. **France 5** broadcasts educational and cultural programs until 7:00 P.M., when it becomes **Arte**, a Franco-German channel showing high-culture programs from its studios in Strasbourg. In 2004, **France 2** had 20 percent of audience share, **France 3** 15 percent, and **France 5** 7.5 percent.

The privately owned networks are **TFI**, which was privatized in 1987 and broadcasts a full range of programs with 31.5 percent of audience share, and **M6,** with 12.5 percent of audience share, which specializes in music programs for younger viewers as well as movies. Reality television has been featured on these two networks with "Star Academy" (similar to "American Idol") on **TFI** and "Loft Story" (similar to "Big Brother") on **M6** attracting huge viewing audiences. Since its launch in 1984, the pay channel **Canal+** has been popular with viewers wanting to watch recent movies, edgy satirical programs like **"Les Guignols de l'info,"** and soccer championship matches. In 2005, **TNT** (**télévision numérique terrestre;** digital television) was introduced when the **CSA** granted licenses for fourteen additional free television channels with targeted programming. Access to these channels is available to everyone by attaching to their television set an adaptor that costs less than 100 euros. For the 75 percent of homes without cable or satellite television, **TNT** increases from six to twenty the number of channels viewers can watch. Pay television via cable and satellite give far greater choice of programs to the other 25 percent. In 2005, a satellite station called **CII** (International Information Channel), involving a partnership between state-run French television and the private **TFI,** was launched. This channel, known in France as **"CNN à la française,"** broadcasting in French and Arabic, is intended to challenge Anglo-Saxon dominance of international television networks and to promote France's language and its view of global affairs.

The number of radio listeners keeps increasing. In 2004, 84.5 percent of the population switched on their radios at least once each day. The state-financed radio network, **Radio-France**, consists of five national radio stations and thirty-nine regional ones as well as an international station, **Radio-France International** (**RFI**). In 2004, the **Radio-France** stations had 31.7 percent of radio listeners. The longest-running, privately owned stations with a full range of programs are, in decreasing order of listener percentages, **RTL** (**Radio Luxembourg**), **Europe 1,** and **Radio Monte-Carlo**. They are today challenged by the privately owned stations that were granted licenses when the state monopoly ended in 1982. In fact, one of these, **NRJ,** is the most listened-to radio station today. Another one, **Skyrock,** is the number two music radio station as well as number one for the generation of listeners aged thirteen to twenty-four.

Unlike in most countries, newspaper readership in France is small, and more advertising is placed in magazines where the readership is larger. National dailies lost 12 percent of their readership between 1997 and 2003. To maintain a diversity of opinion in the press, the state partly subsidizes some small-circulation newspapers such as the Communist national daily, *L'Humanité,* which celebrated its first centenary of publication in 2004. National and regional newspapers tend to align themselves with the views of a political party except *Le Monde,* which is a serious thinking daily that tries to remain independent and is read by the intellectual and managerial classes. *Le Monde; Le Figaro,* which offers conservative views and analyses to its bourgeois readership; and *L'Équipe,* the sports daily, are the three largest-circulation national newspapers, followed by the provocative, left-leaning *Libération,* which was founded after the student revolt that shook France in May 1968. Surprisingly, it is a regional daily, *Ouest-France,* that has the largest circulation. Free daily newspapers in Paris, like *20 Minutes* and *Métro,* have contributed to the declining circulation of the nationals.

The French are the biggest magazine readers in the world. Five national weekly magazines exert considerable influence on opinions, attitudes, and tastes. *Paris Match,* specializing in photojournalism, has the largest circulation. The others are three newsmagazines—the middle-of-the-road *L'Express,* the left-leaning *Le Nouvel Observateur,* and the conservative *Le Point*—and *Le Figaro Magazine,* published in conjunction with the Saturday edition of *Le Figaro.* The top-selling French magazine is the weekly television guide, *Télé 7 Jours.*

In today's news-obsessed world, French habits have changed greatly. The new trend is to consult several news sources. The main ones in 2004 were the 8:00 P.M. television news on **TFI,** the 7:00 A.M.–9:00 A.M. program on radio **RTL**, a newspaper that was bought (*Ouest-France*), a free newspaper or the website of a national daily (*Le Monde*). In 2004, 40 percent of people over eighteen said they surfed the Internet for the latest news.

62. MEN AND WOMEN

The traditional French role for the man was the breadwinner and the one with the power and authority to make family decisions. In the working classes, many women have always worked. (Traditionally, their husbands gave them their paychecks and they were responsible for the family budget). In all classes, women were responsible for the children's education.

In the early 1970s, several laws were passed that significantly improved the independent status of women. In 1975, Simone Veil, the minister for health, championed a new law that legalized abortion and a divorce reform that, for the first time, made it possible to divorce by mutual consent. The previous year, a ministerial post for women's affairs (**Secrétariat d'État de la Condition Féminine**) was established. Françoise Giroud was the first appointee to this post. She proposed that for biological reasons women should seek equivalent rather than identical status with men.

The percentage of women in the workforce has kept increasing. In 2005, 45.5 percent of the workforce were women. However, laws passed in 1972, 1975, 1983, and 2001 establishing equal salaries for men and women have still not been enforced. In 2004, women working in the private and semipublic sectors were, on average, being paid 20 percent less than men. A large percentage of women, having continued their studies to a higher level, want a career in management like men. In 2004, only a third of top management positions were filled by women.

French women were granted the right to vote in 1945. In 1991, the Socialist president François Mitterrand (1916–96) appointed France's first female prime minister, Édith Cresson (1934–). She held office for only ten months, and there has been no female prime minister since. Political parity between men and women was written into the Constitution in 2000, and preferential voting lists drawn up by the left-wing parties for national elections alternate male and female candidates. Women constitute 51 percent of voters, but in 2002, only 13.3 percent of the members of the National Assembly were women. In the conservative government that was appointed ten of the twenty-nine posts were allocated to women. At the local government level, the percentage of women being elected has been increasing. After the 2001 elections, one out of nine mayors were women.

The women's liberation movement in France, **le MLF** (**Mouvement de libération de la femme**) attracted few militant feminists, although the French intellectual Simone de Beauvoir (1908–86) is considered internationally to be one of the founding advocates of women's rights. French women, in winning equivalent status with men, seem to foreign observers to have kept their reputation for femininity and fashionable dress sense.

More French women entering the workforce has influenced family life. Household and family duties have come to be shared to a greater extent, despite the fact that French men, like those of Mediterranean Europe, have been slower than men in northern Europe to share these duties. In 2004, it was estimated that French men spent just under half the time (two hours thirteen minutes) that women spent (four hours thirty-six minutes) doing household tasks.

Male chauvinist attitudes that are slowly changing in many aspects of daily life are not as evident in intellectual discussions, where women's opinions receive the same respect as men's. Men and women from the same social class treat each other as intellectually equal, and discussions are mutual. The lives of one category of women, however, are still dominated by men. In North African immigrant high-rise districts, many women remain the victims of patriarchal, sexist attitudes.

The symbol of the French Republic is a woman, **Marianne**. Her image appears on stamps. In every French city hall (**mairie**), there is a head-and-shoulders statue of her as well as a photograph of the president of France.

63. MONEY

In January 2002, the French national unit of currency, **le franc**, was replaced by **l'euro**. The euro is the shared currency of the twelve countries in the European Union that constitute the Euro Zone. This single currency, which is administered by the European Central Bank in Frankfurt, has meant closer economic integration of the European Union countries. Britain, Sweden, and Denmark have kept their national currencies.

English speakers should remember that in everyday conversation **la monnaie** means change or small coins and not money, which is **l'argent**. "Cash" is **l'argent liquide** or **espèces**. The French still use personal checks to pay for purchases in supermarkets and shops. Checks are accepted with confidence because, under French law, to give a worthless check is punishable by a large fine or imprisonment. The most common credit card is **la Carte Bleue**, which the French also use abroad.

It took some time for the French to accept the use of credit to buy consumer items. The French tradition was to keep as much money as possible in savings (**l'épargne**) and spend it only on essential items. At the same time, the French nurtured a mistrust of the banking system, and it was not uncommon for wealthy peasants and prudent bourgeois to convert savings into gold coin and hide it at home in a woolen sock. These habits gave the French a reputation for being stingy and reluctant to spend money without having compelling reasons. Even today, the French demand value for their money and expect their purchases to last. They may have joined the consumer society, but they haven't joined the throw-away society.

The French are mainly conservative about money and do not flaunt their wealth. The wealthy acquire status and respect among the bourgeoisie by investing their money discreetly in property and cultural artifacts such as antiques, old paintings, and tapestries. Until the 1980s, money was a taboo topic of conversation. During that decade, the fortune amassed by flamboyant entrepreneurs like Bernard Tapie (1945–) with their stock raids and takeovers inspired much media coverage. Their ostentation shocked the conservative French. The recession of the early 1990s saw their fortunes collapse, but the general French attitude toward money and wealth had by then changed. The secrecy that had traditionally shrouded the salaries of top CEOs disappeared with the annual publication in popular newsmagazines of their salaries. While the French remain fascinated by people with a lot of money, being wealthy has become publicly acceptable. Flaunting it is still considered distasteful.

The French are on average three times wealthier today than they were thirty years ago. However, France has a wider disparity in income between rich and poor than most other European countries. Five percent of the population has 50 percent of the nation's private wealth, and the bottom 10 percent has 0.1 percent. Approximately 8 percent of workers are paid the basic wage, **le SMIC** (**Salaire minimum interprofessionnel de croissance**), and, on average, 10 percent of the workforce are unemployed. French taxes are very high because of the cost of financing the welfare state; they absorb about 60 percent of individual income compared with 40 percent in Britain and an E.U. average of 49 percent.

Napoleon Bonaparte (1769–1821) instituted inheritance laws to guarantee the equal rights of heirs, and his laws are still in force. The law dictates that a father's estate be bequeathed to children in equal shares. The law has created a patchwork of the French countryside, especially in prosperous farming areas such as Normandy, for family farms have been repeatedly divided into smaller and smaller plots through inheritance and recombined somewhat randomly through marriage. Another result has been that city dwellers will often own a small lot of inherited land in the country and perhaps a country house that they share jointly with the families of their brothers and sisters.

64. NAMES AND NAME DAYS

France is a traditionally Catholic country, so the majority of its citizens' first names are taken from the Catholic calendar of saints' names. Children traditionally celebrate both their birthday (**anniversaire**) and, although it is becoming rarer, their feast day (**fête**) on the feast of the saint after whom they are named.

Until 1992, state law recommended that children be given a name from a roster of names. Parents being parents, they sought to give their children individuality by forming more original names by hyphenated combinations, such as Marie-Françoise and Jean-Pierre. Some French names, such as Camille, Claude, and Dominique, are unisex. The 1992 law authorizes all first names as long as they are not ridiculous or prejudiced against the child.

The most common French family surnames are Martin, Bernard, Moreau, Durand, and Petit. Dupont, which is frequently treated as the most typical French family surname, actually ranks only fifteenth in frequency.

Since the twelfth century, French children have had the same family name as their father. This changed on New Year's Day 2005, when a law passed in 2002 came into effect allowing newborn children, whether their parents are married or not, to be given the family name of their father, of their mother, or both names joined by a double dash (Martin-- Bernard, for example). Siblings must be given the same family name. This law reflects the fact that 47 percent of French children are today born out of wedlock and removes the stigma from children who had been given their mother's family name because the identity of their father was unknown. Much of the rest of Europe had already complied with the rules established in 1978 by the Council of Europe recommending strict equality between mothers and fathers in transmitting family names.

The particle **de** before a family name indicates that the family belonged to nobility or wishes to give the impression that it did. Adult members of the family usually wear a signet ring stamped with the family crest. Despite France being a Republic, families with a "**de**" name enjoy a certain social prestige. Those descended from noble families that existed before the 1789 Revolution have more prestige than those whose families have bought the title since then. Former President Giscard d'Estaing's (1926–) father acquired the noble title "d'Estaing" in 1922 after proving that his family owned the castle where the d'Estaing family to which he claimed he was related had lived.

65. NUMBERS

French telephone numbers have ten digits, which are not recited singly but in pairs: 01-43-12-95-06, **zéro-un, quarante-trois, douze, quatre-vingt-quinze, zéro six.** The first two digits indicate one of the five zones into which France is divided by France Télécom: **01** is the Paris zone.

France is officially divided into ninety-five administrative districts called **départements.** Each one has a number as well as a name. The numbers correspond to the alphabetical order of the **départements.** For example, the Ain **département** in the Rhône-Alpes region is 01, the city of Paris is 75, and the Val d'Oise **département** in the Paris region in 95. The numbers serve as the beginning of the **département** postal codes and terminate license plate numbers of cars registered in the **département.**

Some handwritten French numerals look different from the corresponding American ones. A French 1 looks like a narrow capital A without the cross bar, and a French 7 is crossed with a bar to avoid confusion with a 1. To Americans, French use of commas and periods in numbers seems reversed. A comma is used to indicate decimals, as in the price €2,30 (two euros, thirty centimes; sometimes written 2€30) or 54,5 **pour cent** (54.5 percent). A period sometimes separates numbers above one thousand into groups of three digits (57.287.212 for fifty-seven million, two hundred eighty-seven thousand, two hundred twelve), although spaces are more common: 57 287 212 (57,287,212).

The street-level floor of a building is called **le rez-de-chaussée,** not the first floor (**le premier étage**), which is the floor above the street level. The French defend their logic by saying that the street level is not a story.

The French observe some conventions in counting days that can cause unwary travelers problems. A week is **huit jours,** and two weeks is

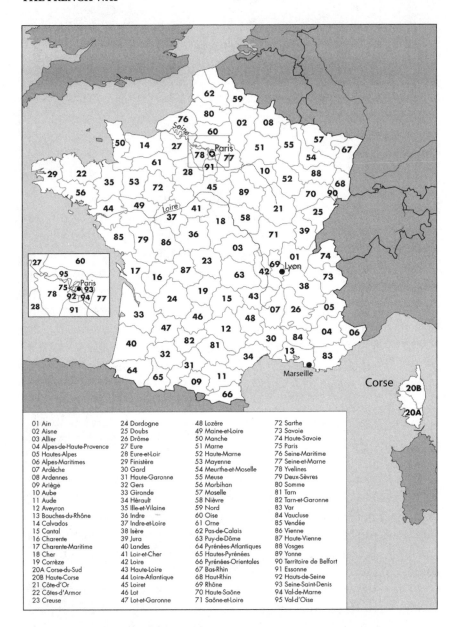

01 Ain	24 Dordogne	48 Lozère	72 Sarthe
02 Aisne	25 Doubs	49 Maine-et-Loire	73 Savoie
03 Allier	26 Drôme	50 Manche	74 Haute-Savoie
04 Alpes-de-Haute-Provence	27 Eure	51 Marne	75 Paris
05 Hautes-Alpes	28 Eure-et-Loir	52 Haute-Marne	76 Seine-Maritime
06 Alpes-Maritimes	29 Finistère	53 Mayenne	77 Seine-et-Marne
07 Ardèche	30 Gard	54 Meurthe-et-Moselle	78 Yvelines
08 Ardennes	31 Haute-Garonne	55 Meuse	79 Deux-Sèvres
09 Ariège	32 Gers	56 Morbihan	80 Somme
10 Aube	33 Gironde	57 Moselle	81 Tarn
11 Aude	34 Hérault	58 Nièvre	82 Tarn-et-Garonne
12 Aveyron	35 Ille-et-Vilaine	59 Nord	83 Var
13 Bouches-du-Rhône	36 Indre	60 Oise	84 Vaucluse
14 Calvados	37 Indre-et-Loire	61 Orne	85 Vendée
15 Cantal	38 Isère	62 Pas-de-Calais	86 Vienne
16 Charente	39 Jura	63 Puy-de-Dôme	87 Haute-Vienne
17 Charente-Maritime	40 Landes	64 Pyrénées-Atlantiques	88 Vosges
18 Cher	41 Loir-et-Cher	65 Hautes-Pyrénées	89 Yonne
19 Corrèze	42 Loire	66 Pyrénées-Orientales	90 Territoire de Belfort
20A Corse-du-Sud	43 Haute-Loire	67 Bas-Rhin	91 Essonne
20B Haute-Corse	44 Loire-Atlantique	68 Haut-Rhin	92 Hauts-de-Seine
21 Côte-d'Or	45 Loiret	69 Rhône	93 Seine-Saint-Denis
22 Côtes-d'Armor	46 Lot	70 Haute-Saône	94 Val-de-Marne
23 Creuse	47 Lot-et-Garonne	71 Saône-et-Loire	95 Val-d'Oise

THE NINETY-FIVE FRENCH *DÉPARTEMENTS*

quinze jours. Therefore, a Eurail pass for **huit jours** is actually valid for only seven days.

66. OVERSEAS DEPARTMENTS AND TERRITORIES

Charles de Gaulle (1890–1970) granted independence to France's last colonies when he returned to power in 1958. The French influence nevertheless remains in the former African colonies of **le Cameroun, le Congo, la Côte d'Ivoire, le Gabon, la Guinée, le Niger, le Mali, la République Centrafricaine, la République démocratique du Congo** (**le Zaïre**), **le Sénégal, le Tchad,** and **le Togo,** and the French for their part maintain policies of cooperation and emotional attachment to those countries.

France has been a leading advocate of the north-south dialogue between the wealthy countries north of the Equator and the developing countries below it to promote the economic development of the latter. France provides technical assistance to the former sub-Saharan French-speaking colonies by sending and paying for technicians, teachers, and other qualified personnel there. In recent years, political instability in some of these countries has forced French expatriates living there to return to France and reduced the number of French companies operating there. In 2004, it was estimated that one hundred thousand French nationals were in these countries.

Certain lands overseas still belong to France. France proper (**la France métropolitaine**), which includes the Mediterranean island of Corsica (**la Corse**), is distinguished from **la France d'outre-mer** (overseas France), which is administratively divided into **départements d'outre-mer** (**DOM**) and **territoires d'outre-mer** (**TOM**).

The **DOM** (overseas departments) are **la Guadeloupe, la Martinique,** and **la Guyane française** in the Carribean, **Saint-Pierre-et-**

THE FRENCH-SPEAKING COUNTRIES OF AFRICA

Miquelon off the coast of Newfoundland in Canada, and **la Réunion** in the Indian Ocean. They have equal status with mainland French **départements** and elect representatives to the National Assembly in Paris. The **TOM** (overseas territories) are **Mayotte** in the Indian Ocean and **la Polynésie française** (Tahiti), **la Nouvelle-Calédonie**, and **Wallis-et-Futuna** in the Pacific Ocean, as well as other minor archipelagoes. Their inhabitants have full French citizenship and elected local governments. Some territories have growing independence movements.

67. PARIS

Since the celebration of the bicentenary of the French Revolution in 1989, France has attracted more tourists annually than any other country. In 2004, more than sixteen million tourists visited Paris, which many claim to be the most beautiful city in the world. Part of the city's beauty derives from its wide avenues, the Seine riverfront, and the height limit of seven stories on its gracious old buildings, which gives most of the city skyline a harmonious appearance. Paris sits on the right (north) bank (**la rive droite**) and left (south) bank (**la rive gauche**) of the Seine. **La Tour Eiffel** (Eiffel Tower), built in 1889 on the left bank, is the international symbol of Paris. It is also the most-visited monument in the world, with sixteen thousand tourists per day.

The center of Paris is the **Île de la Cité**, originally a village established in 200 B.C. by the Parisii, a Gallic tribe, and conquered by the Romans in 52 B.C. The famous Gothic cathedral of **Notre-Dame de Paris** on this island serves as a visual and cultural focal point of the city and is the scene of important national memorial ceremonies. The boulevards interconnect the city's many **places** (roughly, "squares," although they are circular and often have a fountain or a monument in the center of them) that act as neighborhood landmarks and sites of chaotic traffic. The circular **Boulevard Périphérique** separates Paris, with its population of over two million inhabitants, from its suburbs (**les banlieues**). The actual area of Paris, 105 square kilometers, is very small compared with other world capitals like London (1,579 square kilometers).

The underground **métro**, with its numerous stations, makes travel around the city easy for residents as well as for the tourists who come to admire the treasure-filled museums like **le Louvre, le Musée d'Orsay**, and **le Centre Georges-Pompidou**; to wander the historical precincts of the Latin Quarter, **la Bastille, Montmartre**, and **les Champs-Élysées**; to drink coffee in the **cafés** of **St-Germain-des-Prés**; and to dine in the restaurants of **Montparnasse** or shop in the designer fashion boutiques of the right and left banks.

The new business center of Paris is outside the city limits in the western suburb of **La Défense**, whose **Grande Arche**, inaugurated for the bicentenary in 1989, stands at one end of a majestic perspective that passes through **l'Arc de Triomphe** and **la Place de la Concorde** to **le Louvre** at the other end.

By a change in its administrative status, Paris was allowed to elect a mayor in 1977 for the first time since 1871. The **Commune de Paris**, a worker's revolutionary movement, in that year tried to make Paris independent of French government control after the Prussians invaded the city during the Franco-Prussian War. Consequently, for a hundred years, the central government was wary of granting Paris too much autonomy. The Gaullist Jacques Chirac (1932–) was the winner of the 1977 mayoral election, and his administration undertook to make the city cleaner and public services more efficient. Paris was Chirac's power base until he was elected president of France in 1995 and resigned as mayor. The Socialist Bertrand Delanoë was elected mayor in 2001. With the support of the Green Councillors, he pledged to improve the Parisian quality of life by, for example, increasing child-care facilities, improving traffic flow with separate bus lanes, bicycle lanes, and trams that circle Paris on the **Boulevard Périphérique**. In summer, a section of the road along the right bank of the Seine is covered with sand and converted into **Paris Plage** (Paris Beach) for the enjoyment of Parisians.

French government has long been highly centralized, and, despite recent reforms encouraging decentralization, Paris remains the political, administrative, financial, and cultural center of the nation.

68. PARISIANS

Parisians have a reputation for sophistication and for believing themselves superior to all non-Parisians in France and throughout the world. Their candid opinions about the virtues of life in Paris strike many outsiders as arrogance. The stereotypical Parisian sees the entire world as revolving around Paris and awaiting its judgment before adopting new fashions and attitudes. The beautiful atmosphere of light that bathes the city in spring and fall and the elegant nightly illuminations of Parisian monuments and historic facades have given birth to the nickname **la ville lumière** (city of light) for the city; non-Parisians scoff that Parisians commonly misinterpret the name to refer to the intellectual and cultural enlightenment that Paris bestows on the world.

Parisians, of course, are a mixed group of people, as are the people of all major capitals. Their lives are often stressful as they struggle with traffic jams, inadequate housing, crowds, limited facilities for relaxation, and city regulations. Many Parisians maintain strong links with country regions from which they or their families came. The wealthy of the **beaux quartiers** (upper-class neighborhoods) can escape to their weekend country houses and recoup their energies for the next week of hectic Parisian life, but the working classes (whose neighborhoods are under pressure from gentrification) and the large North African population of **Belleville** and **Goutte d'Or** cannot afford weekend retreats and must content themselves with Sunday afternoons walking the streets and sitting in public parks or **cafés**. These poor classes might go to the movies, but they rarely participate in the abundance of cultural activities for which Paris is famous around the world.

There is a growing trend for some married Parisians with young children to leave the stress of the capital to work in large regional towns, which offer a higher quality of family life. However, Parisians, like the French in general, make career moves to other cities and regions much less readily than Americans.

69. POLITENESS AND DIRECTNESS

The French are generally well-mannered and polite. Foreigners sometimes find them rude and dismissive. One reason is the directness and frankness with which the French express their feelings and opinions.

They are accustomed to speaking their minds with each other without fear of offending the listener and expect their listeners to respond with equal candor. Foreigners may also interpret the way the French look at them as challenging because they don't smile; rather, their look is an expression of interest. People watching is a frequent French pastime.

Much attention is given by parents to teaching their children the accepted social codes. With each other, the French are sociable. When they are introduced to someone or when they greet and part from work colleagues each day, they shake hands and exchange polite phrases such as **Bonjour, ça va?** or **Bonsoir, à demain!** Customers entering small shops say **Bonjour, Messieurs-Dames** (roughly equivalent to "Good day, ladies and gentlemen") if there are other customers there, and depart with **Au revoir, Messieurs-Dames. Merci** (thank you) is always acknowledged with **Je vous en prie** or **Je t'en prie** (you're welcome) or the less formal **De rien** (don't mention it). People eating together offer **Bon appétit** (enjoy your meal) at the start of the meal. **Excusez-moi** (excuse me) or **S'il vous plaît** (please) begins a request to an acquaintance for information or to a stranger for street directions. Passing ahead of another person in going through a door or squeezing past in a crowd is excused with **Pardon.** When the French see occasion for personal criticism, the comment is always preceded with an apology, which they see as transforming the criticism into a polite observation rather than a personal attack. Guests invited formally to a French home take flowers or chocolates for the hostess or, if it is an informal gathering, a bottle of wine for the host.

People use professional titles in conversation, when they are applicable, to signify polite respect: **Monsieur le Directeur/Madame la Directrice; Monsieur/Madame le Docteur; Maître** (for an attorney or a famous artist); **Monsieur le Curé/Mon Père/Ma Sœur** (for Catholic religious); **Monseiur le Pasteur** (for a Protestant minister); **Monsieur/Madame le Professeur; Monsieur/Madame le Maire.**

Concerned that a French reputation for rudeness was discouraging the influx of tourist income that makes a significant contribution to the national economy, the government reminds the French to be polite and welcoming to tourists. More French are trying to communicate with tourists in their native languages and not insisting on speaking French with them, as had been their custom. Their willingness to speak English is recognition that English has become the international tourist language.

70. POPULATION

The population of France in the 2004 Census was 62 million: 60.2 million in mainland France (**la France métropolitaine**) and 1.8 million in the overseas departments (**les départements d'outre-mer: la Guadeloupe, la Martinique**, etc.). In mainland France, 23.8 percent of the population was aged under twenty and 21.8 percent was over sixty. In the north and east of France, where traditional industries are disappearing, the population is declining. It is increasing in the south and west. France has the second-largest population in the European Union, which has 456 million inhabitants. Germany has the largest population, but this will decline because the number of deaths each year in Germany is higher than the number of births.

It is predicted that the population of France will increase to seventy-five million in 2050 because of the high birthrate and because there are approximately two hundred thousand more births than deaths annually. The average French birthrate of 1.9 children per woman is one of the highest in Europe (compared to 2 children per woman in Ireland and Iceland but only 1.3 in Germany, Spain, Italy, and Greece). In France, 47 percent of babies are born to unmarried parents, and half of the mothers are aged thirty or over when they give birth. The high birthrate is encouraged by the government policy of granting working mothers twenty weeks of maternity leave for the first child (forty weeks for a third child) with entitlements to 84 percent of salary, free child-care centers (**crèches**), subsidized camps during the school holidays (**colonies de vacances**), tax breaks and family allowances that increase to 300 euros in monthly allowances, and near-free public transport for families with three or more children. Eighty-one percent of French women between ages twenty-four and forty-nine work, including 75 percent of those with two children and 51 percent of those with more than two children. Almost 100 percent of children aged three go to school (**école maternelle**).

In the 2004 Census, 9.6 percent of the population were immigrants aged over eighteen (8.9 percent in 1999). The number of immigrants over age eighteen who took French nationality increased from 37 percent in 1999 to 41 percent in 2004. The immigrant population increases by approximately one hundred thousand annually. The majority of these immigrants are poor and come from France's former African colonies. Immigrant families have more children than French families. France is home to Western Europe's biggest Muslim and Jewish populations. The significant proportion of immigrants in the population combined with the large population shift from the country to the city and the huge decline in church attendance has changed France from a rural, Christian society to a **"black, blanc, beur"** nation (see page 73).

Since the end of the 1960s, the culture and fashions of the younger generation made up of adolescents (**les ados**) and young people up to age twenty-five (**les jeunes**) have had a strong influence on French society. Eighteen is the legal age when young people become adults and can vote. However, because of the difficulty of finding work and the high level of unemployment among those under twenty-five, tertiary students are prolonging their studies and young people are living with their parents longer. Obligatory military service for all young people ended in 2001. It was replaced by a day of "Preparation for Defense" for all young men and women aged sixteen and over.

Les seniors is the term used for the older category of the population. This group is growing rapidly because of the aging of the baby-boomer generation born after World War II and the increase in life expectancy (76.7 years for men and 83.8 for women).

In 2003, one million French citizens became expatriates (30 percent more than in 1991). Fewer are going to live in French-speaking Africa, and 60 percent are going to live in European countries and North America. The most popular countries are Great Britain, Canada, and the United States. The French population in Great Britain has doubled during the last decade but has declined by 40 percent in Germany.

71. *QUEUES* (LINES)

The English may set a world standard for the orderliness of their lines at bus stops, taxi stands, and ticket windows, which they take as a manifestation of their civic responsibility and polite respect for each other. French behavior suggests that they do not accept the English standard in this matter as in so many others.

Despite attempts by public agencies to make people form a single line (**une file d'attente unique**), French lines are disorderly affairs and everyone seems to have a logical, personal reason to break into the line (**resquiller**). Lines publicly demonstrate the single-minded French devotion to individualism and reluctance to acquiesce to any group enterprise that smacks of homogeneity. The French are nonconformists. It is a national pastime to circumvent rules, to find a way around a government regulation or administrative decision, and the name of this national pastime is **le système D**.

The *D* stands for **débrouillard**, which, translated most simply, means "resourceful" but implies a great deal more. The literal meaning of **débrouiller** is "to untangle"; from the French point of view, the chaos of a French line is the logical consequence of a mass of individuals untangling the knotty problem of getting to the head of the line. The French practice **la débrouillardise** in all aspects of life, whether in getting a broken electrical appliance to work, in cutting in lines, or in finding a way to pay less tax. The French compliment **il/elle sait se débrouiller** (he/she knows how to get things done) is always sincere and accompanied with a twinkle in the eye.

72. REGIONALIZATION

France is a highly centralized country, where all major national decisions are made in Paris. The administrative structures are very hierarchical and are organized at five levels: (1) **la commune** (municipality); (2) **le département** (administrative district); (3) **la région** (region); (4) **l'État** (the nation-state); (5) **l'Union Européenne** (E.U.).

At the local level, France is divided into thirty-six thousand **communes**. Each **commune** has a municipal council, which elects a mayor (**le/la maire**). The **communes** are grouped in ninety-five **départements**, whose head is **un préfet** or **une préfète** appointed by the national government. The principal town (**chef-lieu**) of each **département** houses its administrative offices and the **préfet/préfète**. The **départements** themselves are grouped into twenty-two **régions** whose administrative head is a **préfet/préfète de région**, also appointed from Paris. The names of the **régions** correspond to those of the provinces that covered similar areas before the 1789 Revolution, for example, **Picardie, Bourgogne** (Burgundy), **Auvergne, Provence-Alpes-Côte d'Azur**. The French have strong emotional ties to the regions where they were born or, if they were born in Paris and its suburbs, to the regions where their ancestors lived.

The official residence of the president (**le Palais de l'Élysée**) and the seat of the government and its ministries, which constitute the central power of the nation-state, are in Paris. The administrative, political, economic, and cultural prominence of Paris, which has been entrenched for centuries, explains why Paris continues to dominate all aspects of French life. However, with the economic integration of the countries in the European Union, the nation-state lost some of its independence, and the central administration in Paris has had to conform to decisions taken by the European Commission based in Brussels.

President Charles de Gaulle (1890–1970) tried to give more autonomy to the regions, but the referendum of 1969 to approve administrative reforms lost, upon which de Gaulle resigned his presidency. It was not until the election in 1981 of the Socialist president François Mitterrand (1916–96) that a program of decentralization was successfully put into effect. The program provided for elected regional councils with power to make certain financial and local policy decisions without authorization from Paris or the government-appointed **préfet/préfète**. Although this new autonomy was limited, certain regions went about developing their own resources and identity within the European Union, and regional centers such as Lyon and Toulouse grew rapidly as key centers within the European commercial network.

In 2003, an amendment to the Constitution granted more autonomy to the regions, with the state giving the regional councils, which are elected every six years, greater control of regional economic policy. They also have responsibility for regional express trains. The Île-de-France region around Paris is the most densely populated and has the highest economic growth of the twenty-two regions.

Increased regional autonomy is opposed by the "Jacobins," who prefer a highly centralized state and who can point to the many national benefits that have resulted from state planning and control of **grands projets** (major projects), such as the Euro Tunnel under the English Channel, the nuclear power grid, the **TGV** (**train à grande vitesse**), and the Airbus planes.

73. RELIGION

The daily influence of the Catholic Church on everyday life and attendance at Sunday mass, particularly by young people, have declined to the point where the place of religion in France today is mainly cultural. The number of French people who say they are Catholic has fallen from 81 percent in 1986 to 60 percent today, and only 15 percent of these say they practice their religion. Twenty-five percent of the population say they are nonbelievers. However, French history and social traditions are closely bound up with a Catholic identity.

Since Clovis (465–511), the king of the Francs, converted to Catholicism in 496 and made Paris the royal capital, the Catholic tradition has been glorified in abbeys and churches throughout France. The soaring height, devout sculptures, and stained-glass windows of France's medieval Gothic cathedrals are concrete evidence of the fervent religious faith of the twelfth through fifteenth centuries. Catholicism began so early and was so visible in French life that France was called the eldest daughter of the church of Rome (**la fille aînee de l'Église**).

French saints have been some of the most influential in the world. St. François de Sales (1567–1622) reestablished the forgotten principle that salvation was for everyone, not just for the clergy. The charity work of St. Vincent de Paul (1581–1660) among the poor caused a small revolution in French society; his work is continued by his followers in many countries today. Each year, more than five million pilgrims (30 percent of them are Italians) visit the grotto of Sainte Bernadette (1844–79) in Lourdes, an estimated half million of them praying for a miraculous cure of physical disabilities. Sainte Bernadette was a young peasant girl who saw eighteen visions of the Virgin Mary in 1858.

France was one of the first countries to experience the conflicts of the Protestant Reformation in the sixteenth century. The Wars of Religion (1562–98) saw fierce battles between the French Protestants (**Huguenots**) and Catholics. The Edict of Nantes, promulgated in 1598 by Henri IV (1553–1610), the Protestant king who converted to Catholicism to stop the religious fighting, gave Protestants the legal right to practice their religion and granted them certain cities as safe havens. King Louis XIV (1638–1715), seeing the free cities as a threat to the absolute power he was trying to establish, revoked the edict in 1685. One third of the **Huguenot** population emigrated to the Netherlands, Germany, Switzerland, and overseas. Today, 4 percent of the population say they are Protestants, but only one third of them go to church. They reside mainly in the east (Alsace) and the south (Languedoc).

The French Revolution of 1789 attacked the privileges and wealth of the Catholic Church, and the Church and the republican state were adversaries for a century. In 1905, the Third Republic separated church and state by law, defusing the conflict. Since that time, French republics have been constitutionally secular and make no reference to God or religion in state ceremonies. The lay tradition (**la laïcité**) had many vocal adherents among republicans opposed to the church hierarchy, especially among teachers when primary schooling became compulsory for all French children in 1882. State financial aid to private schools (most of which are Catholic) was strongly opposed by supporters of the secular ideology of the Republic, but it is now less a source of controversy. In 2004, to reaffirm the republican principle of public education as secular, a law (**la loi sur la laïcité à l'école**) was passed banning the wearing of all ostensible religious symbols in state schools after Muslim girls began wearing headscarves to school.

The second-largest religion after Catholicism in France today is not Protestantism, but Islam. The growth of Islam is the result of the large number of practicing Muslims among the North African immigrants and their families who have settled in France and have French nationality, as well as among North African immigrant workers. More than a quarter of France's mosques are in and around Paris. Moroccan, Algerian, and Turkish Muslims are the dominant influences in the mosques. The Grand Mosque in Paris is influenced by Algerian Muslims. The mosques elect the members of a national council (**le Conseil français du culte musulman**), which represents Islam in negotiations with the French government.

Jews make up 1 percent of the French population, the highest percentage in Western Europe. More than half live in the Paris region. France has not always been a congenial haven for Jews. Ultranationalist sentiments were quite pronounced in late nineteenth-century France, and these sentiments contributed to unfair conduct in the 1894 trial of a Jewish army officer, Alfred Dreyfus (1859–1935), who was falsely convicted of espionage. Republicans, including the novelist Émile Zola (1840–1902) with his famous public letter "**J'accuse**," fought hard to defend the innocence of Dreyfus, who was finally cleared of all accusations in 1906. Only twenty-five hundred Jews survived from the seventy-eight thousand deported, often with the official complicity of the French Vichy government, during the German occupation (1940–44) of World War II. At the same time, many Jews were secretly offered protection by French non-Jews. Renewed anti-Semitism in this century has taken the form of slogans painted on synagogues and the desecration of Jewish graves.

Since the 1980s, there has been increasing interest in mysticism, in religious sects, and in Buddhism practiced by the growing number of immigrants from Southeast Asia.

74. REPUBLIC

The First Republic in France, founded in 1792, arose after the French Revolution of 1789 in which the middle class, the peasants, and the working class rose against the absolute powers of the monarchy and the excessive privileges of the aristocracy. These events marked the end of the **Ancien Régime** and the beginning of modern democratic France.

The Declaration of the Rights of Man and of the Citizen expressed the guiding principles of the new republic. The declaration embodied the reformist ideals of the eighteenth-century Enlightenment philosophers: equality of all by nature and in the eyes of the law; the obligation of government to guarantee equality, liberty, safety, and property; the separation of legislative, executive, and judicial powers, all forming the basis of good government according to the philosophy of Montesquieu (1689–1755).

The symbolic collapse of the **Ancien Régime** was the fall of the Bastille on 14 July 1789, only seventy-five days after George Washington took office as the first president of the United States under a republican constitution influenced by the very same Enlightenment principles as the French First Republic. In the two countries since, a single republic has formed the government of the United States, but France has lived through five republics, a constitutional monarchy, and two empires. Three of the five republics were heralded by the revolutionary cry **"Aux barricades!"** ("To the barricades!")

The revolutionary tradition established by the 1789 Revolution has been evident in two contemporary outbreaks of civil unrest: the events of May 1968 and the suburban riots of October and November 2005. (See Housing.) A student revolt in May 1968 against outmoded university structures, which raised questions about rigid state controls in general, finally erupted into a general national workers' strike and violent confrontations with police that brought General Charles de Gaulle's (1890–1970) government to the brink of collapse. Salaries were raised, workers gained a voice in workplace decisions, the university system was modernized, and there was a liberalization of social attitudes in many areas of French life, including recognition of feminists and gays. Similar changes had appeared in other Western countries without the violent confrontations. Significant political and social changes in France seem to come about more from explosive ideological conflict than from smooth, gradual change.

The First Republic (1792–1804) lasted until Napoleon Bonaparte (1769–1821) proclaimed the First Empire. Imperial though they were, victorious Napoleonic armies carried the ideals of the Revolution throughout Europe and sowed the seeds for democratic government in much of twentieth-century Europe.

After Napoleon's defeat, a constitutional monarchy reigned until the Second Republic (1848–52) abolished it. Napoleon III (1808–73), in turn, ended the Second Republic and established the Second Empire (1852–70).

Napoleon III was defeated by an invading Prussian army, after a brief war that brought about the first unified Germany in history and the Third French Republic. Germany promptly annexed Alsace and Lorraine, a region that has been the victor's prize whenever Germany and France have opposed each other in a military contest. A working-class insurrection in Paris (**la Commune de Paris**) during the invasion had been intended to establish a more radical government, but the new Third Republic (1870–1940) repressed the movement violently, survived World War I (reclaiming Alsace and Lorraine as the victor in 1918), and saw its political institutions endure until Hitler's military invasion in 1940 during World War II.

The Fourth Republic was established after the end of the war, in 1946. It lasted until 1958, when Charles de Gaulle was recalled to lead France with a new constitution that gave the president more power than Parliament and established the Fifth Republic. Since 1962, the president has been elected in a national election for seven years (since 2000, for five years). The new constitution gave France a stability that continues today.

All five French Republics have paid homage to the democratic principles of the 1789 Revolution, and the republican slogan, **"Liberté, Égalité, Fraternité,"** has become a constant in the rhetoric of all modern French political parties. The traditional conclusion of official presidential addresses to the French people is **"Vive la République! Vive la France!"** ("Long live the Republic! Long live France!") The basis of the French Republic is the assimilation of French-born and immigrant groups into a unified society and a powerful centralized state. Consequently, when French citizens face economic or social difficulties, they turn to the state for help.

Republican sentiment also determines international attitudes. A distinctive and constant feature of French foreign policy is the condemnation of totalitarian regimes that restrict individual liberties and freedom of speech. **"On est en République!"** (We are in a Republic!) is a popular French expression.

75. RIGHTS

The French trace the beginning of their modern country to the Declaration of the Rights of Man and of the Citizen (1789), much as Americans trace theirs to the Declaration of Independence in 1776. The declaration, inspired by the ideas of the eighteenth-century Enlightenment philosophers, granted all French citizens equality in the eyes of the law. The fact that an individual's rights were first enshrined in a Revolutionary declaration could explain why French citizens are quick to assert their individual rights whenever they think they are being threatened.

The frequent use of **"J'ai le droit de . . ."** ("I have the right to . . .") is a reminder that the defense by each individual of his or her rights runs very deep in French behavior. It is also linked to the individualism that is characteristic of this behavior. The expression **"Tu n'as pas le droit (de faire ça)!"** ("You don't have the right [to do that]!") is a spontaneous reaction to loss of dignity as well as a rebuke in many daily life contexts ranging from parents admonishing children to people jostling each other to move forward in a crowd or in a line of impatient drivers trying to cut off other drivers in heavy traffic.

The French carry many official cards and documents that have an official stamp, which they are often required to show to public administration officers. They are proof of the individual's rights as a citizen of the Republic as well as of the special advantages to which they may entitle the holder of the card.

76. SHOPPING

Shopping in France combines the past with the future. Small stores in villages and city neighborhoods and street markets, even in large cities, maintain century-old traditions, while shopping in rural areas now includes huge hypermarkets (**hypermarchés**) on city outskirts. However, the French do not go to shopping malls for leisure as North Americans do. The English word *shopping* has been recently adopted by the French: **faire du shopping** describes the activity of window-shopping and making some purchases.

Neighborhood stores (**petits commerces de proximité**), small specialized stores (**boutiques**), and street markets (**marchés en plein air**) are in many ways the most authentic taste of France. **La boulangerie** (bread bakery), **la pâtisserie** (pastry shop), **la charcuterie** (delicatessen), and **l'épicerie** (grocery) are among the everyday types of stores, with **la boutique de vêtements** (clothes store), **la librairie** (bookstore), and **la joaillerie-horlogerie** (jewelry and clock store) among the more specialized. In these stores, the encounter is a personal one. Customer and shopkeeper exchange greetings as the customer enters and leaves. Initial reaction to supermarkets was negative because the service in them was impersonal.

Conversations at the street markets, usually held twice a week in towns, are likewise personal. The goods sold at these markets (meat, seafood, dairy products, and produce) are often markedly fresher than in the stores, a quality that recommends them highly to the French shopper. Flowers, candy, clothes, and an unpredictable assortment of other items also occupy the stalls. Many towns feature flea markets (**marchés aux puces**), which are similar to the American variety.

Paris has numerous fashion stores with clothes by leading designers. The streets where they cluster, like the **avenue Montaigne** and the **rue du Faubourg Saint-Honoré**, attract many window-shoppers.

Large department stores (**grands magasins**), like **Les Galeries Lafayette** and **Le Printemps** in Paris and **Les Nouvelles Galeries** outside Paris, offer a wide range of merchandise presented stylishly. Chain stores that carry predictable, affordable ranges of clothes and variety goods, such as **Monoprix** and **Prisunic**, flourish in most French towns. Stores are closed on Sunday. In provincial towns they are also closed on Monday and often close for lunch on other days.

Increasingly, shopping centers (**grandes surfaces**) like **Leclerc** and **Intermarché** and hypermarkets (**hypermarchés**) like **Carrefour** and **Auchan** on the outskirts of cities, which offer huge selections, cheap prices, ample parking, and late hours, are forcing small stores to close. Today, French customers make 70 percent of their food purchases in shopping centers. A law has been passed restricting the number of supermarkets and hypermarkets to keep small stores and people in city centers. The hypermarket chain **Carrefour** has opened stores outside France in many countries. The chain of **FNAC** stores, established in 1954, is France's leading "cultural supermarket," selling both high culture (books) and popular culture merchandise.

Two huge companies, **La Redoute** and **Trois Suisses**, produce catalogues that dominate the French mail-order market (**vente par correspondance**). Internet shopping (**e-commerce**) is growing in popularity.

77. SPORTS

France has traditionally sought to lead the world more in intellectual than in athletic achievements. However, changing lifestyles with greater emphasis on fitness (**la forme**) and the influence of major international sporting events like the Olympic Games (**les jeux Olympiques**, or **J.O.**) have made sports more popular leisure activities. At the **J.O.** in Athens in 2004, France came in seventh with thirty-three medals. The main successes were in fencing, equestrian events, and sailing, with seventeen-year-old Laure Manaudou becoming the first French woman swimmer to win at the Olympics. (Paris lost to London as the host city for the Olympic Games in 2012.) Every April, in the Paris International Marathon, one of the largest marathons in the world, athletes run between the Place de la Concorde and the Château de Vincennes.

Two major sporting events announce the arrival of summer. In June, the French Open, tennis's premier clay-court tournament, draws leading world players to the courts at **Roland-Garros** in Paris prior to the famous Wimbledon lawn tennis tournament in London. A French woman, Amélie Mauresmo, achieved number one world ranking in 2004. In July, the world's most celebrated cycling race, **le Tour de France**, attracts huge crowds along the twenty stages of its itinerary around France, preceding the final stage on the Champs-Elysées in Paris. The winner puts on the tour leader's yellow jersey and receives national acclaim. When the American Lance Armstrong won the ninety-second **Tour** in 2005 for a record seventh consecutive time, he became the most successful cyclist in the history of **le Tour**.

The French tend to prefer individual to team sports. Skiing is very popular in the Alps and the Pyrenees. Skiers come from all social classes. Cross-country skiing (**le ski de fond**) is growing in popularity. Snowboarding is popular with the youth culture in winter and windsurfing (**la planche à voile**) in summer. France has the highest per capita number of windsurfers in the world. French sailors, often from Brittany, have been among the leaders in around-the-world and transatlantic yacht races. In 1990, Florence Arthaud became the first woman to win an ocean yachting race and established the record for a solo crossing of the

Atlantic. Since then, national interest and imagination have been aroused by the numerous exploits of adventurous French sailors. In 2005, Vincent Riou won the fifth Vendée Globe yacht race, sailing solo round the world in just over eighty-seven days, and Bruno Peyron and his thirteen crew members set a new round-the-world record of just over fifty days. Also in 2005, after having been the first woman to row across the Atlantic, Maud Fontenoy became the first woman to row solo across the 8,000 kilometers of the Pacific Ocean.

The principal team sports are soccer (**le football**) and rugby (**le rugby**). The national and European soccer championships are watched by enthusiastic fans in stadiums and on television. French soccer achieved cult status in 1998 when France, the host country, won the World Cup, and the French president awarded the winning team members the **Légion d'Honneur** (see Decorations). The winning goal scorer, Zinédine Zidane, who was one of the players of African descent in the team (see Immigration) became a popular hero and was named the best soccer player in Europe in 2001 and 2003. Rugby is most popular in the southwest. The French generally see the European rugby competition, **le Tournoi des Six Nations** (England, France, Ireland, Italy, Scotland, and Wales) as a contest in national pride. France won the competition in 2004 and is the host country for the Rugby World Cup in 2007. English cricket and American baseball have not taken root in France, but basketball is growing in popularity. Golf is a sport for the wealthy. Car racing enthusiasts attend two major events, the 24 Hours at Le Mans and the Monaco rally, and follow the World Formula One championship in which the French carmaker Renault has a team.

Visitors to France will see groups of men playing a type of bowling on gravel surfaces in public parks. This traditional game, called **la pétanque**, is very popular in the south of France.

The fact that the sports newspaper **L'Équipe** is one of the top three national dailies in sales indicates the level of sports involvement by the French as participants, spectators, and armchair analysts.

78. STREET NAMES AND ADDRESSES

Strolling in Paris is itself a cultural experience. A walk through the twenty districts (**arrondisements**) on the left and right banks of the Seine provides reminders of French history not only from the architecture of previous centuries but also from street names. Streets in many French cities and towns carry the names of famous historical figures and events as well as of famous writers, musicians, and artists. The names of some **métro** stations in Paris also recall historical events; others are named after prominent monuments.

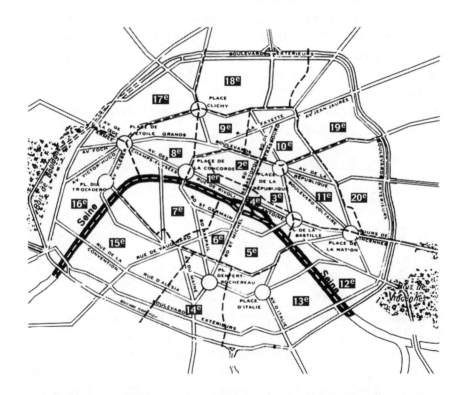

THE TWENTY *ARRONDISSEMENTS* OF PARIS

The French city thus forms a cultural environment for its inhabitants. People may not recall a great deal about some of the events and people in street names, but the signposts remind them of a glorious past upon which the France of today and tomorrow has been built.

Americans accustomed to the predictable grid pattern and numbering of city streets are often disoriented by French streets that do not follow a recognizable geometric pattern and that are called by names, not numbers.

Some streets are named after saints. Tourists using a street directory should remember that all such street names beginning with **Saint** precede those beginning with **Sainte**, which in turn precede any beginning with **Saints**. **Rue Saint-Thomas** thus precedes **rue Sainte-Geneviève**, which precedes **rue Saints-Côme-et-Damien** in a directory. Another distinct feature of French addresses is the use of **bis** and **ter** to insert new addresses between adjacent numbers. Where in the English system, two addresses between 125 and 126 would be styled 125A and 125B, the French would call them **125 bis** and **125 ter**. (French concertgoers, incidentally, will cry **"Bis!"** to encourage an encore, not "Encore!" The encore performance is similarly **un bis**.)

79. TIME

The French have their own concept of punctuality. It is well illustrated by the apology they frequently use when they arrive very late: **"Mieux vaut tard que jamais"** ("Better late than never"). It is accepted behavior to arrive a little late for a personal appointment or a reception. When invited for a dinner at home, guests are expected not to arrive until at least ten minutes after the specified time and can arrive up to half an hour late without causing irritation to their hosts. However, the many French who travel by train get to the station punctually because the French national railway system has an enviable reputation for its trains leaving and arriving on time.

The French tend to separate their lives into periods of work and periods of pleasure. Periods of pleasure have a certain sanctity, especially mealtimes. Schools have a two-hour lunch break. In provincial towns, there is a two-hour lunch break. In Paris and the larger provincial cities, the lunch break has been reduced to one hour because workers now have to travel longer distances and cannot go home for lunch. The evening meal is eaten after 7:00 P.M. and often at 8:00 P.M. to coincide with the nightly television news broadcast. The usual time specified for formal invitations to dinner is 8:30 P.M. Personal phone calls are made between 8:00 A.M. and 9:30 P.M.

The duration of the official working week is thirty-five hours. Workers working more than thirty-five hours per week are compensated with extra leave days called **RTT** (**réduction du temps de travail**). All salaried workers are officially entitled to five weeks of annual paid vacation. The annual summer vacation traditionally lasts one month and breaks the year into two parts. These are further broken by short vacations in winter, often spent skiing, and the long weekends of **Toussaint** (1 November) and **Pâques** (Easter).

The rhythm of the year for the majority of the population is influenced by the school calendar, which begins in September (**la rentrée**) and finishes in June with the **baccalauréat** exams, when pupils begin a two-month vacation. During the school year, there are one- or two-week vacations at **Toussaint**, at Christmas (**Noël**), in February (winter) and in April (spring). The beginning dates of these vacations are staggered between the three zones into which French schools are divided so as to avoid overcrowding at vacation destinations.

Most national museums are closed on Tuesday. The others are closed on Monday.

The French calendar week begins on Monday rather than Sunday. The expressions **huit jours** (eight days) and **quinze jours** (fifteen days) mean "a week" and "a fortnight." The word **prochain** (next) used with a weekday does not mean "in the next week" as it does to some English speakers. For example, **vendredi prochain**, when spoken on a Wednesday, means the Friday two days away, not the Friday nine days away. Wednesday is a day off for primary school children and a half day for high school students; on the other hand, both go to school for a half day on Saturday.

Since 1991, some primary schools have been officially allowed to adopt a four-day week with no classes on Wednesday or on Saturday morning. This gives pupils a full weekend. The school year for these schools begins a week earlier to make up the time lost by no Saturday classes.

80. TRANSPORTATION

The French train system is run by a government-owned company called **SNCF (Société Nationale des Chemins de Fer Français)**. French trains are renowned for their speed and punctuality. The first high-speed train, the **TGV (train à grande vitesse)**, was introduced in 1981 between Paris and Lyon. The **TGV Méditerranée**, introduced in 2001, travels from Paris to Marseille in three hours. **TGV** trains now serve most major destinations in France and, in 2003, carried their one billionth passenger. Their comfort and speed make them very popular and a direct competitor with internal airlines. The **TGV** technology was purchased by Spain, by South Korea, and for the Houston–Dallas–San Antonio line.

Paris has six major train stations, each one serving a different region of the country. Trains from the **Gare de Lyon**, for example, go south to Marseille, the **Côte d'Azur**, and Italy, while those from the **Gare de l'Est** serve Strasbourg and Germany and those from the **Gare Montparnasse** serve Brittany and the southwest.

The underground railways in Paris, Lyon, and Marseille are called **le métro**. In Paris, travelers can reach all parts of the city quickly because of the frequency of the trains, the 293 stations, and the numerous points (**correspondances**) for changing lines. **Métro** travel is also very economical, especially with the discounted books of tickets (**carnets de billets**). One journey, no matter how long or short, costs the same price with one ticket.

A fast train system called the **RER (Réseau Express Régional)** has extended the **métro** network to the outer suburbs of Paris, including Versailles and the Charles de Gaulle international airport at Roissy.

In Paris and other major cities, there is a network of public buses (**autobus**) and, in some of them, modern trams (**tramways**).

In 2005, Paris was the busiest air hub in the world. The French aviation company **Air France** amalgamated in 2004 with the Dutch company **KLM** to become the European leader. The first flight of the supersonic Concorde from Paris to Rio de Janeiro in 1976 brought international prestige to the French aeronautical industry. The Concorde flights across the Atlantic by Air France and British Airways ended in 2003.

Today, the city of Toulouse in southwest France is the headquarters of the aeronautical industry under the control of EADS (European Aeronautic Defense and Space Company). EADS is an aerospace consortium in which France and Germany have an equal 30 percent share, the other partners being Great Britain and Spain. Sixty percent of the activity of EADS is the construction and marketing of the very successful Airbus planes, which are assembled at Toulouse-Blagnac. Since 2001, aircraft sales for Boeing have lagged behind Airbus. The Airbus 350 and the superjumbo A380, which supersedes the Boeing 747 as the world's biggest passenger plane, have been sold to many international aviation companies. The Paris Air Show (**Salon du Bourget**), held every two years, is the European showcase for the aviation industry.

Shipbuilding has been another success story for French transportation engineering. The British luxury ocean liner, *Queen Mary 2*, the world's largest, was built and launched from the shipbuilding yards at Saint-Nazaire on the Atlantic coast in 2003.

A large fleet of barges (**péniches**) carries raw and manufactured materials on France's extensive network of rivers and canals. Some barges also carry foreign and French tourists for tours of the more scenic canals.

81. URBAN AND RURAL LIFE

France has a population of more than sixty-two million but is one of the least densely populated countries in Europe. Because 90 percent of the

French population lives in urban or semiurban areas and 20 percent in the **Île de France** region around Paris, large areas of the diverse country landscape offer unspoiled vistas of fields, forests, valleys, and mountains.

The French population has moved rapidly from the country to urban agglomerations since World War II. In 1946, 38 percent of the total workforce was farmers; today only 3.5 percent of the French live on family farms. Agriculture now accounts for just 2 percent of the gross domestic product (GDP), half the figure of twenty years ago. (Incidentally, in the predominantly urban society that France has become, services now constitute more than 50 percent of the GDP.) The suburbs (**les banlieues**) of major cities grew as the countryside emptied. This also means that many of today's urban residents are within a generation of one rural area or another and its traditions, and many contemporary Parisiens identify themselves, for example, as **Bretons** or **Normands** rather than **Parisiens**—that is, they continue to identify themselves with the region from which their family came.

The influx of country dwellers to cities and towns needed housing, as did immigrant workers who arrived in large numbers, mainly from **le Maghreb** (Morocco, Algeria, and Tunisia). Government-financed, low-cost apartment buildings called **HLM (habitations à loyer modéré)** were erected in the suburbs. Low-income workers from the city have increased the suburban population as rents rose in their old neighborhoods under the economic pressure of gentrification. **HLM** buildings are now often socially deprived concentrations of people with high unemployment, especially among the young and immigrants. The current pattern is for high-income earners to live in the city center and low-income earners in the suburbs, which is the opposite of the American pattern.

Individual housing developments were built in the outer suburbs around the "New Towns" planned by government and urban architects to decrease inner-city overcrowding resulting from the baby-boomer population. More recently, the increasing influence of the French ecology movement on ways of life and the growth of e-working (**le télétravail**) have encouraged a trend to return to country life. People influenced by these factors live on the outskirts of the suburbs, where they can enjoy both a rural and an urban life. They are called **rurbains**.

Since the 1980s, government reforms have given greater power to regional councils, and provincial cities have enjoyed a new growth cycle as a result. Regional economic growth was also stimulated by managers and other workers who abandoned the stress of Parisian life in search of a higher quality of life. The **TGV** (**train à grande vitesse**) network has reduced the isolation of provincial cities by making travel between them and Paris faster. Thirty-five urban agglomerations outside Paris hold more than one hundred thousand people each. The five largest are, in order, Lyon, Marseille, Lille, Bordeaux, and Toulouse.

A French survey in 2005 to determine in which city life is best classified cities in terms of housing, leisure possibilities, employment, culture, educational institutions, and dynamism. The top five were Lyon, Toulouse, Bordeaux, Nantes on the Atlantic coast, and Tours on the Loire River.

During the time agriculture made the greatest contribution to France's wealth, life in country villages was prosperous and conservative. With the decline of the rural population, many of these villages are today virtually empty except for the houses bought by city dwellers as **résidences secondaires** for weekends and vacations or by Europeans (mainly British and Dutch) attracted by the low cost of the houses and the French lifestyle.

The nationalist and conservative values of the rural society continue to exert an influence on the national psyche out of all proportion to its percentage of the population and its economic importance. Forty-five percent of the E.U. budget goes to agriculture and 25 percent of this goes to subsidies for France. Farmers' demonstrations against changes to the generous subsidies of the **PAC** (European Union Common Agricultural Policy) receive widespread popular support. The administrative division of France into thirty-six thousand **communes**, each with an elected mayor and council, gives more importance to rural than urban communities and thus ensures the endurance of traditional rural values.

82. VACATIONS

The Socialist **Front Populaire** government of 1936 introduced a law mandating two weeks of paid annual vacation (**congés payés**) for all salaried workers. The law is often cited in France as a watershed in the progress of the working class toward an improved lifestyle. The paid annual vacation was increased to three weeks in 1956, to four weeks in 1969, and to five weeks in 1982. Many workers in special categories now receive six weeks of paid vacation every year. Germany is the only country in the world where the average annual vacation is longer than in France.

Most French people take their vacations in July and August, and many industrial plants close for the whole month of August. The first wave of crowds leave Paris and the north of France after the national holiday of 14 July and seek out the sun and beaches of the Mediterranean and Atlantic coasts. The second and largest wave departs on 1 August. On 15 August, a third wave leaves on vacation, while those who left in mid-July throng home. During the last weekend in August, all roads and trains from the south to the north groan with the crowds returning home. In September, people resume their work or schooling (**la rentrée**), and life returns to normal after the national pause for summer vacation.

Many people use their fifth and sixth weeks of vacation to go skiing in the winter or to take other short trips. Twenty-seven percent of French people take several vacations a year, while for other Europeans the figure is 19 percent. The introduction of the thirty-five-hour working week in 1999 gave workers extra leave days called **RTT** (**réduction du temps de travail.**) Many workers choose to use these days to take long weekends that the wealthier spend visiting tourist cities in Europe. Some workers now have up to eleven weeks of vacation and leave time a year. However, with less money to spend on vacations, they are staying at home instead of traveling.

Eighteen percent of people taking their vacation in July and August 2004 went to countries outside France, with Spain, Italy, Portugal, and Morocco being the most popular. Seventy-two percent stayed in France: 48 percent went to a beach, 33 percent to country locations where varied landscapes and cultural treasures are strong attractions, and 16 percent went to the mountains. The percentage of the population leaving home for a summer vacation has declined from 63 percent in 1997 to 52 percent in 2004. This can be explained by the worsening economic situation and high unemployment. Seventy-two percent of people in the liberal professions went on vacation, 54 percent of white-collar workers, 48 percent of blue-collar workers, and 22 percent of farmers. Classified by age, the younger generations form the majority of those vacationing away from home in July and August: 63 percent of those aged fifteen to twenty-four; 56 percent of those aged twenty-five to thirty-four; 61 percent of those aged thirty-five to forty-nine; 45 percent of those aged fifty to sixty-four; 32 percent of those over sixty. There is a tendency for the latter group to vacation outside this period when prices are lower.

People who want to spend a low-cost vacation in the countryside can go to **un gîte rural** (countryside accommodation). The association **Gîtes de France**, which celebrated its fiftieth anniversary in 2005, has fifty-six thousand farmhouses whose owners welcome paying guests. Ecological vacations (**le tourisme vert**) are increasingly popular.

A proliferation of summer arts festivals, particularly in towns and historical sites south of the Loire River, draws large crowds. The theater and dance festival in Avignon and the music festival in Aix-en-Provence also draw many foreign visitors. Other people who want their vacation to be more intelligent than idle sunbathing (**le bronzage idiot**) on the beach choose the Club Méditerranée, which began in 1950 with resorts in France. Today, there are ninety-eight Club Med villages across the world, offering cultural and sports activities and opportunities for self-improvement at their facilities.

France's share of the world tourism market was 11 percent in 2003, and tourism constituted 6.7 percent of the GDP. France is the most popular tourist destination in the world, especially for the British, the Germans, and the Dutch. The Germans have an expression: "To be as happy as God in France." After France, Spain; the United States; Italy; and China are the most popular tourist destinations, in that order.

83. *VIVE LA DIFFÉRENCE!*

"Vive la différence!" which imitates the patriotic slogan **"Vive la France!"** ("Long live France!"), has become the catch cry for France's uniqueness in a globalized world dominated by the United States. The protection of France's specific cultural identity was first expressed through the concept of **exception française** (French exception) when President François Mitterrand declared that cultural works are not merchandise and France successfully led opposition to the American proposal to include cultural products in the 1993 General Agreement on Tariffs and Trade (GATT).

France was thus able to continue its policy of protecting and subsidizing its national movie, television, and popular music industries against American cultural imports. The French government imposes an 11 percent tax on American movies and uses these funds each year to finance two hundred French films, of which fifty must be made by new directors. Despite this, in 2004, 47.2 percent of tickets sold to French moviegoers were to see American films, compared to 38.4 percent to see French films. French films made up only 20 percent of DVD sales. On French public television, 35 percent of movies shown are American. By law, French public television is required to have 60 percent of the films shown to be European and 40 percent of other programming to be French. The same law, from 1989, requires a minimum of 40 percent of songs played on French radio to be in French. The initial concept of **exception française** evolved into **exception culturelle française** and then into the present policy of **diversité culturelle** (cultural diversity), by which France proclaims the right of every country to protect its national culture against what is called "American cultural imperialism" and to promote a dialogue of cultures that respects all.

In 2005, delegates of the UN Educational, Scientific and Cultural Organisation (UNESCO) voted 148 to 2 to ratify a treaty to protect cultural diversity from global conformity that for many delegates is represented by Hollywood, Big Macs, and Coca-Cola. This treaty gives countries the right to implement measures to protect the diversity of cultural expressions on their territory. Cultural expressions include movies, music, art, language, and ideas as well as cultural activities, goods, and services. The United States and Israel opposed the treaty. Films and music are among the United States' largest exports. In 2004, the foreign box-office take for American movies was $16 billion.

Since the collapse of the Berlin Wall in 1989 and the disintegration of the Soviet Union, the United States is the undisputed world super-power. France's policy of cultural diversity is both a cultural and political reaction to American-led globalization (**mondialisation**). The French do not reject globalization but resist Anglo-American models of it. The robust French tradition of state intervention in the national economy conditions France to want a global market with rules and institutions to enforce them, as opposed to a self-regulated market economy. In France, the United States confronts the only country that has always seen itself as endowed with a universal mission and that is determined to champion cultural diversity in the new world order.

84. WORK AND UNEMPLOYMENT

In contrast to the United States, where a free-market economy dominates, the French economy is primarily state regulated. It is not only driven by grand, state-supported projects (**grands projets**) like the **TGV**(**train à grande vitesse**), Airbus, and nuclear energy, but the state remains the majority shareholder in some key companies as well and is also a massive employer in public services like education, health, and transportation.

The workforce is divided between the public sector and the private sector. In the public sector, workers, called **fonctionnaires** (civil servants), are paid by the state. Unlike workers in the private sector, they have employment security and guaranteed retirement pensions. These benefits are envied by workers in the private sector, where the average wage is lower and the risk of unemployment is greater.

The state, which employs more than 25 percent of the workforce, is a major player in workplace relations. The government sets the basic hourly wage rate, called **le SMIC** (**salaire minimum interprofessionnel de croissance**). In 2005, the minimum wage was twelve hundred euros a month. Other decisions result from negotiations between the government, the trade unions (**syndicats**), and the chief employers' federation **le Medef** (**Mouvement des entreprises de France.**) For the first time, a woman, Laurence Parisot, was elected president of **le Medef** in 2005. The national influence of the trade unions is not matched by their membership. Only 8.2 percent of French workers are trade union members. This is the lowest membership rate in Europe.

The three main national trade unions are: **la CGT** (**Confédération générale du travail**), the oldest union, which was founded in 1895 and was officially affiliated with the Communist Party until 2003; **la CFDT** (**Confédération française démocratique du travail**), the largest union, which was founded in 1964, has a center-left orientation and is more willing to reach agreement with the government; and **FO** (**Force Ouvrière**), founded in 1948, which is apolitical. In 1992, **la CFDT** became the first union to elect a woman as its leader, Nicole Notat. Other unions represent particular professions, such as farmers and teachers. Today, the unions have become the voice of protest in French society and combine to organize the many street demonstrations and strikes that disrupt French life. These protests receive broad public support because in the French social model, which is based on state-centered solutions, the unions' defensive action to protect workers' rights is an appeal to social solidarity, a fundamental value to which the French are attached.

In 1999, a thirty-five-hour workweek was introduced by the Socialist government in an attempt to promote the creation of new jobs and thus reduce unemployment (**le chômage**). Unemployment increased from 2.7 percent of the working population in 1972 to 12.6 percent in 1997. Despite plans by both left-wing and right-wing governments to reduce unemployment, it has remained at around 10 percent since then. In 2005, 63 percent of the working population in France had employment, compared with 72 percent in Great Britain.

Persistent high unemployment in France has been paralleled by a decline in permanent employment in the private sector, where workers are more likely to be offered a short-term contract (**un CDD,** or **contrat de durée déterminée;** or **un CNE,** or **contrat nouvelle embauche**) than a permanent contract (**un CDI,** or **contrat de durée indéterminée**). In 2005, 20 percent of workers had **un CDI.** French labor laws make part-time work less common in France than in other European countries. A recent trend is for unemployed young French people to go to Great Britain, where there is more part-time work.

There has been increasing feminization of the workforce since the 1970s, as educated, middle-class women have joined the high percentage of women from the lower classes who had always been in the workforce. Eighty-one percent of French women between the ages of twenty-four and forty-nine work, but serious inequalities continue to exist between women's and men's wages. The high rate of unemployment has particularly affected women and young people. In 2005, 22.9 percent of those under age twenty-five were out of work. Unemployment has also affected managerial workers (**les cadres**). To find work, job seekers register with the **ANPE** (**Agence nationale pour l'emploi**), which was established by the government in 1967. The legal retirement age for workers is sixty, though workers in some special categories may retire at a younger age.

A political consequence of high unemployment has been increased support for the extreme-right National Front and the rise of nationalism. Workers who used to vote for the Communist Party have been recruited to the National Front by its claims that restricting the number of North African Arab immigrant workers would translate to more jobs for the French.

The French government has a generous welfare policy for those who are unemployed. Some commentators say that this policy does not encourage the unemployed to seek new employment. High unemployment has produced a large proportion of people living below the poverty line (6.1 percent of the population) and a considerable group of homeless people (**SDF,** or **sans domicile fixe**).

France is the sixth-largest economic world power. Eight of the 100 largest world companies are French. Carrefour is the second-largest merchandiser in the world behind Wal-Mart, and Sodexho is the world's largest service company. Despite these successes, high unemployment and job insecurity, combined with rising levels of poverty and the marginalization of jobless youth, pose a serious threat to social cohesion, which is one of the pillars of the French Republic. There is a widening gap between the wealthy upper classes (**la France d'en haut**), who look to the future with confidence, and the poorly paid and unemployed (**la France d'en bas**), who feel dispossessed and excluded from the nation's prosperity.

85. WORLD WARS AND COLONIAL WARS

Germany declared war on France on 3 August 1914. World War I developed into a trench war (1915–17) between the combined French and Allied forces and the German army in the north of France. The French won the Battle of Verdun in 1916, but only after suffering severe loss of human life. An armistice was signed on 11 November 1918, after American forces joined the Allied forces. One quarter of young French males died in the war (nearly 1.5 million French soldiers died in all), and this greatly restricted both France's economic recovery and its population growth for decades.

Germany under Hitler was again at war with France in 1939, when World War II began. In 1940, the French army collapsed before the German tank offensive and, on 25 June the eighty-four-year-old Marshal Philippe Pétain (1856–1951), the new leader of the French government, signed an armistice with Germany. The Nazi army occupied outright the entire north of France and the Atlantic coastline while the south was given nominal independence with its capital at Vichy. General Charles de Gaulle (1890–1970) broadcast a patriotic call from London on 18 June (**L'Appel du 18 juin**), urging the French not to collaborate with the Nazis because "France has lost a battle! But France has not lost the war!" He organized the Free French movement outside of France. Jean Moulin (1899–1943) and others organized the French Resistance movement within Vichy France. On D-Day (**Jour J**), 6 June 1944, Allied forces made up of 1.7 million British, 1.5 million American, and 220,000 soldiers of other nationalities under the command of General Dwight D. Eisenhower landed on the coast of Normandy to liberate France. Paris was liberated on 25 August 1944, and the war in Europe ended on 8 May 1945. General de Gaulle and those in the Resistance were war heroes, and Marshal Pétain was condemned to prison for treason. Other major Vichy collaborators were summarily executed or imprisoned after court trials. Some notorious war criminals were not convicted, because of an ambivalent attitude among many French about Vichy policies. Reconciliation between France and Germany was enshrined in a Friendship Treaty signed in 1963 by President Charles de Gaulle and Chancellor Adenauer. This treaty established the parameters for the close cooperation of the two countries, which has been a feature of the strength of the European Union. In a survey, on the eve of the sixtieth anniversary of D-Day in 2004, asking the French who are their surest allies, 82 percent responded the Germans, 65 percent the British, and 55 percent the Americans.

In 1946, France became embroiled in a war for independence with its colony of Indochina. This war ended in 1954 with the humiliating defeat of the French army by Vietminh forces at Dien Bien Phu in Vietnam. France then withdrew from Vietnam and was replaced by the United States.

The same year that France accepted defeat in Vietnam, the North African French territory of Algeria began a war for independence. The two other French protectorates in North Africa, Morocco and Tunisia, had been granted independence without contest, but Algeria had not. Algeria was unique in having been integrated into the administrative structure of mainland France, and a significant part of the population was French. It was difficult for the army and, indeed, for much of mainland France to accept an independent Algeria. In 1958, President René Coty (1882–1962), fearing a civil war between supporters of a French Algeria and supporters of an independent Algeria, recalled General de Gaulle to form a new French government. De Gaulle first granted independence to all French African colonies that wished for it and then negotiated a cease-fire between the French army and the forces for independent Algeria. In 1962, Algeria received its independence. France continues to maintain a special relationship with Algeria, Morocco, and Tunisia (**le Maghreb**).

France endured seventeen years of colonial war after World War II before finally achieving peace. The baby-boomer generation began entering the workforce to fill the gap created by those who died during World Wars I and II, and France began thirty years of uninterrupted economic growth (**les trente glorieuses**), which ended in 1974 with the first oil crisis.

86. *X*

X is the colloquial name for the **École Polytechnique**, which specializes in advanced mathematics and physics. In the nineteenth century, mathematicians were known as the **X**. The **École Polytechnique** was founded in 1794 as a school for engineers of public works. In 1804, Napoleon Bonaparte (1769–1821) gave it the status of a military school, which it still retains. The students wear a uniform and a two-cornered hat. Women were first allowed to enroll in 1972. **X** and the **École Nationale d'Administration** (**ENA**), which was founded in Paris in 1945 by Charles de Gaulle (1890–1970) and is now located in Strasbourg, are the most prestigious higher-education institutions in France, and graduates of these two schools readily find appointments to the top ranks of industry and the civil service. The French have a particular reverence for the elite **Grandes Écoles** and their graduates. Admittance to them is by a very difficult competitive examination (**un concours**), which top students take after two years of special preparatory classes following the **baccalauréat**.

The graduates of **l'ENA**, called **énarques**, have a virtual monopoly on all significant government positions. Presidents Valéry Giscard d'Estaing (1926–) and Jacques Chirac (1932–) and most prime ministers since the 1980s have been **énarques.**

X is also used to designate someone you don't want to name or a person or persons unknown; for example, **Monsieur X** or, in the legal expression, **porter plainte contre X** (to bring a court case against an unknown person or persons).

87. XENOPHOBIA

One of the main reasons the extreme right-wing National Front Party, led since 1972 by Jean-Marie Le Pen (1928–), became increasingly popular in the 1980s was its anti-Arab immigrant policy. Le Pen got 14.4 percent of the vote in the first round of France's 1988 presidential election. In the 2002 presidential election, he received 17 percent in the first round, more votes than the Socialist prime minister, Lionel Jospin. This qualified him to be the opponent of President Jacques Chirac in the second round. The conservative Chirac, supported by the left-wing parties, which opposed the National Front ideology, won with 82 percent of the vote.

Le Pen's theme "France for the French" found a receptive audience among unemployed workers, who had been used to voting Communist, and among former supporters of conservative parties, who were disappointed by the feebleness of their parties' defense of the French identity of France.

Le Pen and his supporters blamed Arab immigrants for working in jobs that unemployed French workers could fill. They conveniently forgot that these jobs went begging until the Arabs arrived to do them. They also attacked as un-French the immigrants' continued practice of their Muslim religion. Violent and antisocial behavior by unemployed Muslim youths in the public housing projects that are mainly inhabited by Arab and African immigrants on the outskirts of big cities has contributed to a general public feeling of insecurity, which attracted further support for the National Front.

The **beurs**, that is, French-born children of North African immigrants who have French nationality, founded an antiracist association called **SOS-Racisme** with encouragement from the Socialists. **SOS-**

Racisme organized concerts that attracted large crowds of young people who opposed Le Pen's racist campaign. The association's emblem is the open hand of friendship with the slangy slogan **Touche pas à mon pote!** (Hands off my pal!)

The adopted heroine of the National Front is Joan of Arc, who liberated France from foreign occupation by the English in the fifteenth century. Each year on 10 May, the Feast Day of Joan of Arc, the National Front organizes a huge parade to her statue in Paris. Young skinheads in the parade have assaulted Arabs who happened to be in their path.

Support for the extremist ideology of the National Front is also one of the explanations for the increase of anti-Semitism in France, with Jewish cemeteries being desecrated and the walls of synagogues painted with racist slogans. The French president always publicly denounces these anti-Semitic acts and the rise of intolerance.

88. YOUNG PEOPLE

The baby-boomer generation began with the huge rise in the birthrate after World War II. Since then, young people (**les jeunes**) have been an influential group in French society. Forming a larger percentage of the population, **les jeunes** became the trendsetters and the catalysts for change in a society that had been conservative and traditional.

A major turning point was the events of May 1968 (**les événements de mai**), which began with students (**les étudiants**) protesting the overcrowding of university lecture halls and the outdated curriculum. Their protest movement evolved into a national strike of all workers that brought the country to a standstill and contributed significantly to the resignation of President Charles de Gaulle in April 1969.

Since their successful revolt in May 1968, university students have organized many street demonstrations (**manifestations** or **manifs**) and sit-ins (**occupation des lieux**) and each time forced the government to withdraw or amend proposed reforms that would change long-established university traditions. Most notable among these traditions is the right of every student who passes the **baccalauréat** examination to enroll at a university. Students pay no course fees. High school students (**les lycéens**) began joining the demonstrations in the 1980s when a Socialist government proposal for the state education system to control private schools caused huge controversy. The proposal was withdrawn and, since then, high school students have been active participants in student demonstrations. In 2005, they led the protests against a government proposal to include a component of continuous assessment in the grades given for the **baccalauréat** examination.

Education is a constant preoccupation of French families because the grades their children get at secondary school determine their subsequent prospects for higher education, their employment possibilities, and their hopes for a successful life. High rates of youth unemployment (22.9 percent of under-twenty-five-year-olds in 2005) put further pressure on young people to succeed at school. Equality of opportunity for all pupils, no matter what their socioeconomic background, is the loudly proclaimed goal of the French education system. However, this goal, rarely achieved by working-class children in comparison with children of the bourgeoisie, has become unattainable with the huge influx into the schools of children from immigrant families. Among the graduates from the **Grandes Écoles** (see Education), which form the elite of French society, less than 1 percent are working-class children, whereas 63 percent are children of parents who are executives or have a liberal profession.

Today, the education system is failing in its role of integrating the children of immigrant families into a cohesive society that respects the values of the Republic and state institutions. It is, in fact, producing two distinct groups: those who succeed at school, go on to higher education, and find employment (they come mainly from the bourgeoisie), and those who fail at school and face long-term unemployment. The majority of those who fail are **beurs**, children of immigrant parents from North Africa, living in suburban **cités** (housing projects). This inequality among French citizens and the widening economic gap between the haves and the have-nots have generated a growing feeling of injustice and alienation among the latter.

Furthermore, a new underclass made up of unemployed young people, mainly male Muslim youths who are second-generation immigrants with French nationality, has emerged and they are creating their own rules of violence and criminality in the **cités**. They were the leaders of the suburban riots in October and November 2005, defying the authority of the state, which they claimed no longer guaranteed the equality of all its citizens. This violent outbreak of civil unrest highlighted the failure of the immigration policy of assimilation, of the education system, of town planning in the suburbs, and of the economy to provide employment. President Chirac called it **"une crise d'identité nationale"** (a national identity crisis). The euphoria of **"black, blanc, beur"** France (see Immigration) after winning the World Soccer Cup in 1998 had evaporated.

In France, young people legally become adults at age eighteen and are entitled to vote. Voting is not compulsory. Because the young people form a large segment of society, they have a strong influence on fashion and cultural trends. They have been more open to American pop culture than their parents and to educational and economic opportunities in the European Union. Students from France are one of the largest national groups to participate in the **Erasmus** program that enables university students to study in another European country for a period of three months to one year. Most of these students, however, come from the bourgeoisie. Successful rap singers and bands from the **beur** culture are popular with young people from other social groups who listen to **Sky-rock** and FM music stations for the young.

The baby-boomer generation is now reaching retirement age. Consequently, the percentage of **les seniors** in the population is increasing and the percentage of **les jeunes** declining. Despite this, because France has one of the highest birthrates in the European Union, the social and cultural influence of **les jeunes** will remain important.

89. ZAPPING

Television viewers frequently zap between programs. The French also apply **le zapping** to a trend in French behavior to shift rapidly from one fashion to another, from one attitude to another, or from one romantic partner to another.

The French now enjoy greater professional mobility and have more contact with social and regional groups outside their own. The European passport and the euro currency make it easier to go to other European countries and encounter their values and behaviors. The millions of tourists coming to France as the world's number one tourist destination, as well as multinational companies establishing offices and plants in France, bring with them different world perspectives. The younger French generations travel outside France and make foreign friends more frequently than did their predecessors.

These changes, together with the increased choices of a consumer society and more sophisticated advertising techniques, help explain why **zapping** has become a feature of French behavior.

90. *ZUT!*

This frequent French exclamation, which often becomes **"Zut, alors!,"** expresses frustration and exasperation. It is a polite expression used by all social groups, whereas the somewhat equivalent **"Merde!,"** often heard in colloquial conversation, is considered impolite.

The exclamation **"Bof!"** expresses indifference to an idea or project. If a French person replies **"Bof!"** with a shrug of the shoulders to a proposal, you know not to expect any enthusiasm. **"Super!"** or **"Génial!"** expresses an enthusiastic response.

USEFUL WEBSITES

The following websites provide information spanning a broad spectrum. They enable readers to read further, view related images, and research in more detail. These sites are designated (E) for English, (F) for French, and (E, F) where both options are available. Sites are selected for their interest and stability, but inevitably some addresses will have become dead links since publication.

Government Sites
- **lessites.service-public.fr** for links to the wealth of French national Internet sites; search by topic or name of governmental organization (E, F)
- **insee.fr** see *La France en Faits et Chiffres* for statistics and articles on population, work, health, education, the economy, social life; articles and figures can be selected by region; see *Le Portrait de Votre Région* for data, maps (F)
- **france.diplomatie.fr/culture/france/biblio** see *thèmes* for contemporary art, comics, international relations, philosophy, photography, or soccer; see *textes* for literary works; see *poésie* for a poetry anthology; see *revues* for journal descriptions (F)

City Guides

In addition to official city sites, these guides cover multiple cities.

- **lecity-guide.com** guides to what's going on across France (F)
- **viamichelin.fr** travel itineraries, maps, hotels, restaurants (E, F)
- **voyager-en-france.com** guide to thirty-one cities (E, F)

French Search Engines

- **francite.com**
- **ifrance.com**
- **lycos.fr**
- **mageos.com**
- **nomade.aliceadsl.fr**
- **voonoo.net**
- **wanadoo.fr**
- **fr.yahoo.com**

Educational Sites

- **utm.edu/departments/french/french.html#history** Tennessee Bob Peckham's Globe-Gate project, with extensive links to history, education, books, maps, culture, media, language, and daily life websites in French and English (E)
- **web-guide-fr.com/France/index.html** links to sites for government bodies, media, shopping, and services (F)
- **about.com** a network of guides that includes *France for Visitors*, *French Language*, and *French Cuisine*, as well as French-related material within general topics such as *Art History*, *Architecture*, etc. (E)
- **aatf.utsa.edu/surfing.htm** links proposed by the American Association of Teachers of French (E)

INDEX

ABOUT THE AUTHOR

Ross Steele has published extensively on contemporary France, on the French newsmagazine *L'Express*, and on the teaching of French culture. He is Honorary Associate Professor of French at the University of Sydney, Australia, and is a member of the Editorial Board of *Modern Language Journal*.

The Governor-General of Australia awarded him the Centenary of Federation Medal in 2001 and in 2006 made him a Member of the Order of Australia (AM) for "service to tertiary education, particularly the promotion of French language and culture in Australia, and to the community through support for a range of arts organisations."

Ross Steele has been honored with three awards by the government of France for international promotion of French language and culture: *Chevalier de la Légion d'Honneur, Officier de l'Ordre National du Mérite,* and *Officier des Palmes Académiques.*